M000188544

RICH
and
THIN

MCGRAW-HILL

New York   Chicago   San Francisco   Lisbon   London
Madrid   Mexico City   Milan   New Delhi   San Juan
Seoul   Singapore   Sydney   Toronto

DEBORAH McNAUGHTON
and MELINDA WEINSTEIN

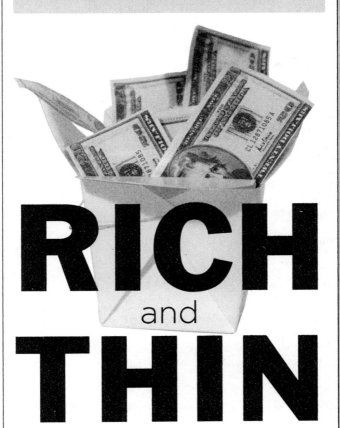

RICH
and
THIN

Slim Down, Shrink Debt, and
Turn Calories into Cash

1 2 3 4 5 6 7 8 9 0   DOC/DOC   0 9 8 7

ISBN-13: 978-0-07-149414-4
ISBN-10: 0-07-149414-6

Library of Congress Cataloging-in-Publication Data

McNaughton, Deborah
  Rich and thin / by Deborah McNaughton and Melinda Weinstein.
    p. cm.
  ISBN 0-07-149414-6 (alk. paper)
  1. Finance, Personal. I. Weinstein, Melinda. II. Title.

HG179.M2515 2007
332.024—dc22   2007001179

Contents

Introduction

AS WE SAT OUT AT OUR favorite fast food restaurant, eating a feast of chicken sandwiches and french fries, we started to contemplate, "How much is this lunch really costing us?" We knew the prices—$2.99 for each chicken sandwich and $1.59 for each order of french fries—but how much would this one lunch cost us over 1 year, 5 years, even 10 years? Not to mention the calories we are consuming. We checked our Money Calorie Counter for the answer. What a shock! One chicken sandwich was 660 calories and the accompanying french fries 460. If we consumed a chicken sandwich and fries (or similar fast food) five times a week, it would be equivalent to 291,200 calories per year, or 83 pounds. The cost would be $1,190.80 per year. But if we put that money in a mutual fund account for 5 years, we would have saved $7,684.34, in 10 years, we would have $20,327.45; in 20 years, $75,354.70. One of us, Deborah, has published two previous books, *Financially Secure* and the *Get Out of Debt Kit*. These titles touched lightly on the Money Calorie Counter, and they garnered much public interest. Even the media was intrigued with the concept.

So, we knew the topic of money, weight, and wealth touched a nerve. *Rich and Thin* gets the message out!

In this book, the coauthors—Deborah and daughter Melinda—have joined forces to help readers like you build personal wealth by becoming aware of everyday purchases. This book is also an eye-opener to the world of dining, take-out, fast food, gourmet coffee and other non-food habits. That said, we don't intend to give health or dieting advice, nor is it an investing guidebook. *Rich and Thin* will help you to focus on your spending habits as they relate to those little daily indulgences, revealing that a habit of a donut and coffee a day can be keeping you from a fat bank account and a great physique.

In creating the Money Calorie Counter, we set out on a calorie safari and visited all kinds of restaurants around the country, collecting calorie information on the most popular meals and drinks. What an eye-opener!

Before we forge ahead into the principles of the book and reveal the Money Calorie Counter, we should tell you a bit about ourselves.

DEBORAH'S STORY

Having personally experienced a financial crisis many years ago, and being $300,000 in debt, my husband and I made some pretty poor decisions that almost cost Melinda her life when I let our medical insurance lapse. Melinda had emergency brain surgery and almost died. The great news is she survived the surgery with no side effects and the hospital picked up the bill from a trauma fund for children. My husband and I did emerge from many years of debt and poor financial management a bit scarred, but much wiser. And I became a crusader for financial health; my mission is to help others earn money, build wealth, and make smart financial and credit decisions. My husband and I never filed for bankruptcy, but we restructured our lives with sacrifices and settled our accounts with creditors. The effort took years, but we won that battle and are now financially secure and reaching out to others. Over the years, Melinda has gained extensive experience in the financial and mortgage industries, so it was only logical that we co-author this book. As a mother-daughter team, we both bring different insights. (Besides, Melinda was a good sport, visiting all the restaurants and fast food stops, since she could afford more of the calories than I could. You should have heard the stories she came back with and the food she dumped in the trash when she was told the calorie count, not to mention the fat content!)

WEIGHING IN

Money, personal wealth, and weight go hand in hand. Every year, the top New Year's resolutions are to lose weight, get out of debt, save more money, and give more to religious organizations and charities. *Rich and Thin* shows you how to have the best of all possible worlds. You will be able to use the information in it as you watch your calories and think about how to use your money productively. Obviously, you have to eat; please don't starve yourself just to save money. Just use wisdom and moderation—and we'll help you to do just that. Brown-bag healthy lunches, and get a handle on your personal addictions. Food is not the only addiction people have, so we've included several nonfood addictions in the book as well.

In these pages, we address two topics that are constantly on people's minds: money and health. Life would be a whole lot easier if our bank accounts grew and our waistlines stayed in the lower-digit range. Unfortunately, for most of us, the opposite holds true. This book will help you achieve your goal of getting out of debt, saving money, and losing a few pounds. Not only will it show you how to cut back on your calorie intake, but it will also help you identify other addictions, save money, set a manageable budget, shrink your debt, enjoy life, and share your wealth. And our Money Calorie Counter will get you on your way. It's funny how we love and crave chocolate, potato chips, ice cream, pizza, and other high-calorie, great-tasting items, and blame those cravings on a variety of things: depression, anxiety, stress, and financial crises are just a few of the culprits cited. By and large, we are a society that eats too much food—most of it fatty or sugary—and moves around too little. But you can unite your self-improvement efforts, and battle the bulge while building personal wealth. In the chapters that follow, we'll open your eyes to your damaging habits, and help you to find creative ways to change your eating and spending habits—and ways to enjoy that growing bank account.

PART ONE

Find Money, Not Calories

1

Everyone's Money Dream

WE ALL HAVE DIFFERENT definitions of personal wealth. Yours may be to have substantial investments and assets. Or it may be to have enough money to feel comfortable. Being able to pay your bills on time, get the things you want, and have a nest egg for retirement may be your definition of wealth. Whatever your definition is, you need to remember: money doesn't grow on trees.

You can't build wealth without hope and a dream. You can't depend on that *big* deal to fall in your lap and bring you wealth. It doesn't happen that way. That's a terrific dream, but it's not reality. In order to make your financial dream come true, you need to take action. But that can be a daunting prospect, leaving you feeling like you are a hamster, running on the wheel and going nowhere. The first step in confronting your financial situation is to start moving in the right direction and jump off that wheel. That is where the Money Calorie Counter, featured in Chapter 2, comes in. Once you take close stock of where you are and where you want to be, the Money Calorie Counter will help you to put your good intentions into action.

What does "wealth" really mean to you? One way to establish what wealth is in your world is simply to specify what it is you want in life. Perhaps your list looks like this:

- Savings for retirement
- College fund
- Home ownership
- Money to pay bills
- Luxuries
- A second car
- Investments: real estate, stocks, mutual funds, etc.
- Being able to contribute to charitable organizations
- Being healthy and fit

In order to achieve these goals, both monetarily and physically, you first need to identify the obstacles keeping you from being healthy and wealthy. As you read through the chapters in Part One, you will begin to see a pattern that many people fall into with regard to their spending habits. The simple truth is that you can't obtain wealth as long as you spend recklessly. The added benefit of the Money Calorie Counter is that you will immediately see how many calories you can eliminate from your diet while curbing your spending. Now, don't take this exercise so seriously that you stop eating; just use good judgment in how you can curtail your spending *and* cut some calories out of your diet. What kinds of changes can you make? You may take more trips to the grocery store (where it is almost certain to cost less) instead of the gourmet shop for your special coffee. Or you could substitute lower-priced packaged baked goods at the supermarket for those designer bagels and other goodies from the high-priced bakery. By learning what your weaknesses are you will be able to begin saving in both your diet and your wallet. Throughout the book, we will be showing you how to painlessly set up a workable budget while putting money away and watching it grow. Your new budget will put you on the path to getting out of debt. Excessive debt will stop your wealth-building efforts in their tracks. For most people, debt is like a noose around their necks. Many people fret and lose sleep worrying about it. Debt can only slow the wealth-building process, because all your financial endeavors are focused on coming up with ways to eliminate it. With the strategies taken from this book, you should be able to devise a game plan for breaking the "debt trap," become debt free, and direct your efforts toward gaining wealth.

With the easy-to-follow strategies in this book, you have a greater chance of gaining wealth and building your savings, because you'll finally understand exactly what complex financial jargon really means and how you can use the systems in place to make wise financial decisions. Check out Chapter 7, "Grow Your Money, Not Your Waistline," to find innovative ways to make your money grow; it provides terrific examples of how compounding interest impacts savings, and you'll find out how to apply the magic of compounding interest to your own finances.

You are never too old to begin saving. You may have started later than you hoped by working to reduce your debt and barely surviving just your daily living expenses, but you can start to fulfill your financial dreams now!

Related to debt is how to build good credit. Chapter 8, "Build Wealth with a Healthy Credit Report," is one of the most important chapters in the book. Your credit report says it all. A credit report can determine what interest rate and costs you will have to pay if you purchase a home, investment property, an automobile, or any other secured item. It also will determine if you can rent that apartment, get the best rates on your insurance, or secure the job of your dreams. A good credit report will help you gain greater wealth from your investments. This chapter will show you how to understand your FICO ("Fair Isaac Corporation") score, and tips to keep your credit report looking great.

Part of wealth involves flaunting those little luxuries. You don't have to flaunt a flashy car or sparkly jewelry or even the latest electronic devices to feel good about what you've been able to accomplish. Wealthy people are those who can have the taste of luxury and know that they have worked hard to build their investments, savings, and retirement savings without splurging and creating new debt. They are debt free from credit cards, loans, and other things, and they have made sacrifices to obtain what they have. Chapter 10, "Mmm ... A Taste of Luxury," will show you how to walk the walk and talk the talk. Nothing is more disheartening than seeing people who appear to have everything but who can barely afford their mortgage because their credit cards are maxed out, they have no savings, and they are paying huge car payments, all to achieve the image of having wealth. Remember, you can't judge a book by its cover, and that pertains to people as well. Our book will empower you to do it right and remain true to yourself.

One of the greatest blessings that people can do for mankind is to give money to a charitable organization. It may be a church or charity, a person in need, maybe a family member who is hurting financially. Open your eyes and you will see unlimited opportunities to be in a position to make charitable contributions. Part of the Money Calorie Counter program is the ability to eliminate the obstacles to gaining wealth and giving more freely to others.

Life is a journey. There will be different times and seasons in your life. At one time your finances might be strong; at another they might be challenged. Remember, you have the power to change your destiny. The financial decisions you make today can impact future decisions and your financial outcome tomorrow. Now let's get started to a wealthier and trimmer you by first completing your wish list. Keep the list close by and refer to it often to make your dreams a reality.

WISH LIST

List your financial wishes below. If you are married, complete this list with your spouse.

1. _____

2. _____

3. _____

4. _____

5. _____

6. _____

7. _____

8. _____

9. _____

10. _____

11. _____

12. _____

13. _____

14. _____

15. _____

16. _____

17. _____

18. _____

19. _____

20. _____

2

Money Calorie Counter

MONEY AND FOOD ARE inextricably linked together; it takes money to buy food: fast food, junk food, pleasure food, tasty food, or whatever kind of food makes you feel good. And, by the way, these are the foods that tend to put on the weight. If we were to tell you that the Café Mocha that you must have every day before work, five days a week, at $3.35 per cup would ultimately cost you $871 and 104,000 calories per year (that equates to 30 pounds), would you think twice about spending your money and packing on the pounds? How about that donut to go along with the mocha? The donut costs $0.69 per donut, which is $179.40 per year, and the calories would total 46,800—that's equal to 13 pounds per year. So, if you are starting every morning with a mocha and donut, you are spending $1,050.40 ($871.00 annual mochas plus $179.40 annual donuts) per year, not to mention the potential 43 pounds you might gain (obviously weight gain differs per person, but you get our point).

Think about the debt that could be paid off with that $1,050.40. Or the personal wealth that could be gained by investing that money. Let's take this one step further. If you were to take the money that you would be spending each day and put it into an investment each month that would yield an interest of 10 percent, instead of giving in to a daily habit, in five years you would have saved $5,620.64; in 10 years you would have saved $14,868.33; and in 20 years you would have saved $55,117.52 using the mocha example above. Likewise, with the donut, in five years you would have saved $1,157.68; in 10 years you would have saved $3,062.43; and in 20 years, $11,352.56.

Assume that a large order of fries costs $1.79. There are 620 calories in one large order (not to mention all that fat). If you ate an order of fries five days a week, the annual cost would be $465.40. The calories would be 161,200. Let's go a step further. If you took the annual savings ($465.40) from the fries and put it into a mutual fund that was earning 10 percent interest compounded monthly, in five years you would have $3,003.27; in 10 years you would have $7,944.57 in savings; and in 20 years, $29,450.85. The incredible thing is also that the calories per year that you're avoiding amount to 161,200. This equates to 46 pounds. Amazing, isn't it?

The Money Calorie Counter gives a whole new perspective on saving money, building personal wealth, losing inches, and keeping your weight down. You can fatten up your savings while trimming down your physique. As you look at the Money Calorie Counter, find the foods and beverages that are your Achilles' heel. The numbers shown are based on a scenario of an individual eating a selection of these items five times during the week. The chart will show you how many calories can be saved plus how much money you can yield for your retirement savings and increase your bank account if you deposit the savings monthly into an investment that will yield 10 percent interest compounded for 5 years, 10 years, and 20 years.

While we realize it's unlikely you would eat the exact same thing day in and day out, the charts illustrate the impact your dieting can have on your wallet in both the short and long term. The trick to this type of savings and calorie reduction plan is not simply to avoid making the purchase or to cut back from the daily expense but also to take the money you would be spending on the item and put it into an interest-bearing investment vehicle such as a mutual fund.

As you review the tables in this chapter, you will see that we assumed you are eating and drinking the same thing every day, which for some of you may not be the case. However, we are trying to show you that if you are spending an equivalent amount each day, by investing that amount you could have a sizeable nest egg down the road as well as little or no debt. All calculations are based on five days per week and 10 percent interest compounded monthly in a mutual fund or a similar interest-bearing investment deposited monthly.

Prices and calories in the Money Calorie Counter were collected from the major food chains. The prices and calories shown are the median prices and calories gathered in our research.

The calculations were based on 5 days per week, which equates to 260 days a year.

Once you've identified your own food weakness, complete the Money Calorie Counter worksheet to see where your money and calories are going.

MONEY CALORIE COUNTER

Fast Food

| Item Name | Cost | Srv | Calories | | Pounds | | Yearly Cost | 10% Interest Compounded Savings | | |
			Month	Year	Mth	Yr		5 Years	10 Years	20 Years
Bacon & Cheese Baked Potato	$2.49	580	12,567	150,800	4	43	$647.40	$4,177.73	$11,051.39	$40,967.95
Bacon Swiss Crispy Chicken Sandwich	$3.39	760	16,467	197,600	5	56	$881.40	$5,687.75	$15,045.86	$55,775.64
Baked Potato w/ Broccoli and Cheese	$2.49	540	11,700	140,400	3	40	$647.40	$4,177.73	$11,051.39	$40,967.95
Baked Potato w/ Butter & Sour Cream	$1.49	500	10,833	130,000	3	37	$387.40	$2,499.93	$6,613.08	$24,514.96
Bean Burrito	$0.79	370	8,017	96,200	2	27	$205.40	$1,325.46	$3,506.26	$12,997.86
Beef Burrito	$1.99	550	11,917	143,000	3	41	$517.40	$3,338.83	$8,832.23	$32,741.45
Beef 'N Cheddar Sandwich	$2.89	480	10,400	124,800	3	36	$751.40	$4,848.85	$12,826.71	$47,549.15
Beef Soft Taco	$0.79	210	4,550	54,600	1	16	$205.40	$1,325.46	$3,506.26	$12,997.86
Beef Taco	$0.69	170	3,683	44,200	1	13	$179.40	$1,157.68	$3,062.43	$11,352.56
Beef Taco Salad	$3.29	850	18,417	221,000	5	63	$855.40	$5,519.97	$14,602.03	$54,130.34
Beef Tostada	$0.99	250	5,417	65,000	2	19	$257.40	$1,661.03	$4,393.92	$16,288.46
Breaded Chicken Sandwich	$2.89	582	12,610	151,320	4	43	$751.40	$4,848.85	$12,826.71	$47,549.15

| Item Name | Cost | Calories | | | Pounds | | Yearly Cost | 10% Interest Compounded Savings | | |
		Srv	Month	Year	Mth	Yr		5 Years	10 Years	20 Years
Caesar Side Salad (no dressing)	$1.99	45	975	11,700	0	3	$517.40	$3,338.83	$8,832.23	$32,741.45
Caesar Side Salad	$0.99	70	1,517	18,200	0	5	$257.40	$1,661.03	$4,393.92	$16,288.46
Charbroiled BBQ Chicken Sandwich	$2.99	290	6,283	75,400	2	22	$777.40	$5,016.63	$13,270.54	$49,194.44
Charbroiled Chicken Salad	$3.39	200	4,333	52,000	1	15	$881.40	$5,687.75	$15,045.86	$55,775.64
Cheese Quesadilla	$1.49	500	10,833	130,000	3	37	$387.40	$2,499.93	$6,613.08	$24,514.96
Cheeseburger	$1.49	370	8,017	96,200	2	27	$387.40	$2,499.93	$6,613.08	$24,514.96
Cheeseburger (quarter pound)	$3.19	530	11,483	137,800	3	39	$829.40	$5,352.19	$14,158.20	$52,485.04
Cheeseburger with bacon	$2.79	727	15,752	189,020	5	54	$725.40	$4,681.07	$12,382.88	$45,903.85
Chef Salad	$3.99	150	3,250	39,000	1	11	$1,037.40	$6,694.43	$17,708.85	$65,647.44
Chicken and Cheese Quesadilla	$2.39	580	12,567	150,800	4	43	$621.40	$4,009.95	$10,607.56	$39,322.65
Chicken Bacon 'N Swiss Sandwich	$3.29	610	13,217	158,600	4	45	$855.40	$5,519.97	$14,602.03	$54,130.34
Chicken Breast Sandwich	$2.89	540	11,700	140,400	3	40	$751.40	$4,848.85	$12,826.71	$47,549.15
Chicken Burrito	$2.39	560	12,133	145,600	3	42	$621.40	$4,009.95	$10,607.56	$39,322.65
Chicken Caesar Wrap	$3.99	610	13,217	158,600	4	45	$1,037.40	$6,694.43	$17,708.85	$65,647.44
Chicken Finger 4-pack	$3.59	640	13,867	166,400	4	48	$933.40	$6,023.31	$15,933.53	$59,066.24
Chicken Finger Salad (no dressing)	$4.99	570	12,350	148,200	4	42	$1,297.40	$8,372.24	$22,147.16	$82,100.43
Chicken Nuggets (6 pieces)	$2.29	290	6,283	75,400	2	22	$595.40	$3,842.17	$10,163.73	$37,677.35
Chicken Sandwich	$2.99	660	14,300	171,600	4	49	$777.40	$5,016.63	$13,270.54	$49,194.44
Chicken Soft Taco	$1.39	190	4,117	49,400	1	14	$361.40	$2,332.15	$6,169.25	$22,869.66
Chili—large	$1.79	300	6,500	78,000	2	22	$465.40	$3,003.27	$7,944.57	$29,450.85
Chili—small	$0.99	200	4,333	52,000	1	15	$257.40	$1,661.03	$4,393.92	$16,288.46

Item Name	Cost	Srv	Calories Month	Year	Pounds Mth	Yr	Yearly Cost	10% Interest Compounded Savings 5 Years	10 Years	20 Years
Chili Cheese Fries (large)	$2.19	357	7,735	92,820	2	27	$569.40	$3,674.39	$9,719.89	$36,032.05
Chili Cheese Fries (regular)	$1.69	299	6,478	77,740	2	22	$439.40	$2,835.49	$7,500.74	$27,805.56
Chili Cheeseburger	$1.29	350	7,583	91,000	2	26	$335.40	$2,164.37	$5,725.42	$21,224.36
Combo Burrito	$1.89	530	11,483	137,800	3	39	$491.40	$3,171.05	$8,388.40	$31,096.15
Corn Dog	$0.99	262	5,677	68,120	2	19	$257.40	$1,661.03	$4,393.92	$16,288.46
Crispy Chicken Sandwich	$3.19	550	11,917	143,000	3	41	$829.40	$5,352.19	$14,158.20	$52,485.04
Curly Fries Large	$1.69	620	13,433	161,200	4	46	$439.40	$2,835.49	$7,500.74	$27,805.56
Curly Fries Medium	$1.39	400	8,667	104,000	2	30	$361.40	$2,332.15	$6,169.25	$22,869.66
Curly Fries Small	$1.19	310	6,717	80,600	2	23	$309.40	$1,996.59	$5,281.59	$19,579.06
Double Cheeseburger	$3.69	1,020	22,100	265,200	6	76	$959.40	$6,191.09	$16,377.36	$60,711.54
Double Hamburger	$3.29	920	19,933	239,200	6	68	$855.40	$5,519.97	$14,602.03	$54,130.34
Fish Sandwich	$2.19	530	11,483	137,800	3	39	$569.40	$3,674.39	$9,719.89	$36,032.05
French Dip Sandwich	$3.19	440	9,533	114,400	3	33	$829.40	$5,352.19	$14,158.20	$52,485.04
French Fries— large	$1.79	620	13,433	161,200	4	46	$465.40	$3,003.27	$7,944.57	$29,450.85
French Fries— medium	$1.59	460	9,967	119,600	3	34	$413.40	$2,667.71	$7,056.91	$26,160.26
French Fries— small	$1.29	290	6,283	75,400	2	22	$335.40	$2,164.37	$5,725.42	$21,224.36
French Fries with cheese (large)	$1.89	322	6,977	83,720	2	24	$491.40	$3,171.05	$8,388.40	$31,096.15
French Fries with cheese (regular)	$1.39	265	5,742	68,900	2	20	$361.40	$2,332.15	$6,169.25	$22,869.66
Fried Zucchini	$1.69	320	6,933	83,200	2	24	$439.40	$2,835.49	$7,500.74	$27,805.56
Garden Salad	$1.49	50	1,083	13,000	0	4	$387.40	$2,499.93	$6,613.08	$24,514.96
Grilled Cheese Sandwich	$1.29	282	6,110	73,320	2	21	$335.40	$2,164.37	$5,725.42	$21,224.36

| Item Name | Cost | Calories | | | Pounds | | Yearly | 10% Interest Compounded Savings | | |
		Srv	Month	Year	Mth	Yr	Cost	5 Years	10 Years	20 Years
Grilled Chicken Caesar Salad	$2.99	100	2,167	26,000	1	7	$777.40	$5,016.63	$13,270.54	$49,194.44
Grilled Chicken Salad (no dressing)	$4.99	230	4,983	59,800	1	17	$1,297.40	$8,372.24	$22,147.16	$82,100.43
Grilled Chicken Sandwich	$3.79	400	8,667	104,000	2	30	$985.40	$6,358.87	$16,821.19	$62,356.84
Hamburger	$0.99	320	6,933	83,200	2	24	$257.40	$1,661.03	$4,393.92	$16,288.46
Hamburger (quarter pound)	$2.39	430	9,317	111,800	3	32	$621.40	$4,009.95	$10,607.56	$39,322.65
Hot Dog	$1.09	240	5,200	62,400	1	18	$283.40	$1,828.81	$4,837.76	$17,933.76
Hot Dog with cheese	$1.59	366	7,930	95,160	2	27	$413.40	$2,667.71	$7,056.91	$26,160.26
Hot Dog with chili	$1.09	290	6,283	75,400	2	22	$283.40	$1,828.81	$4,837.76	$17,933.76
Hot Dog with chili and cheese	$1.59	330	7,150	85,800	2	25	$413.40	$2,667.71	$7,056.91	$26,160.26
Hot Dog with kraut	$1.09	260	5,633	67,600	2	19	$283.40	$1,828.81	$4,837.76	$17,933.76
Hot Dog with mustard	$0.99	260	5,633	67,600	2	19	$257.40	$1,661.03	$4,393.92	$16,288.46
Hot Dog with relish	$1.09	270	5,850	70,200	2	20	$283.40	$1,828.81	$4,837.76	$17,933.76
Mexican Pizza	$2.39	390	8,450	101,400	2	29	$621.40	$4,009.95	$10,607.56	$39,322.65
Mexican Rice	$0.79	190	4,117	49,400	1	14	$205.40	$1,325.46	$3,506.26	$12,997.86
Mozzarella Sticks	$2.49	470	10,183	122,200	3	35	$647.40	$4,177.73	$11,051.39	$40,967.95
Nachos	$1.00	380	8,233	98,800	2	28	$260.00	$1,677.80	$4,438.31	$16,452.99
Nachos (large)	$1.19	440	9,533	114,400	3	33	$309.40	$1,996.59	$5,281.59	$19,579.06
Onion Rings (large)	$1.79	507	10,985	131,820	3	38	$465.40	$3,003.27	$7,944.57	$29,450.85
Onion Rings (regular)	$1.49	331	7,172	86,060	2	25	$387.40	$2,499.93	$6,613.08	$24,514.96
Pintos 'n Cheese	$0.79	180	3,900	46,800	1	13	$205.40	$1,325.46	$3,506.26	$12,997.86
Roast Beef Salad	$4.49	120	2,600	31,200	1	9	$1,167.40	$7,533.34	$19,928.00	$73,873.93

Item Name	Cost	Srv	Calories		Pounds		Yearly Cost	10% Interest Compounded Savings		
			Month	Year	Mth	Yr		5 Years	10 Years	20 Years
Sour Cream & Chives Baked Potato	$0.99	370	8,017	96,200	2	27	$257.40	$1,661.03	$4,393.92	$16,288.46
Southwestern Wrap	$3.99	590	12,783	153,400	4	44	$1,037.40	$6,694.43	$17,708.85	$65,647.44
Steak Soft Taco	$1.49	190	4,117	49,400	1	14	$387.40	$2,499.93	$6,613.08	$24,514.96
Turkey Salad	$4.49	90	1,950	23,400	1	7	$1,167.40	$7,533.34	$19,928.00	$73,873.93

Sandwiches

Item Name	Cost	Srv	Calories		Pounds		Yearly Cost	10% Interest Compounded Savings		
			Month	Year	Mth	Yr		5 Years	10 Years	20 Years
Avocado & Turkey Sandwich	$4.49	675	14,625	175,500	4	50	$1,167.40	$7,533.34	$19,928.00	$73,873.93
BLT Sandwich	$2.79	581	12,588	151,060	4	43	$725.40	$4,681.07	$12,382.88	$45,903.85
Chicken Club Sandwich	$3.49	675	14,625	175,500	4	50	$907.40	$5,855.53	$15,489.69	$57,420.94
Club Sandwich	$3.59	370	8,017	96,200	2	27	$933.40	$6,023.31	$15,933.53	$59,066.24
Ham & Swiss Cheese Sandwich	$3.39	410	8,883	106,600	3	30	$881.40	$5,687.75	$15,045.86	$55,775.64
Hot Ham and Swiss Cheese Sandwich	$3.29	530	11,483	137,800	3	39	$855.40	$5,519.97	$14,602.03	$54,130.34
Hot Pastrami Sandwich	$4.49	705	15,264	183,170	5	52	$1,167.40	$7,533.34	$19,928.00	$73,873.93
Italian Meatball Sandwich	$3.79	500	10,833	130,000	3	37	$985.40	$6,358.87	$16,821.19	$62,356.84
Pastrami Reuben Sandwich	$4.49	875	18,967	227,604	6	65	$1,167.40	$7,533.34	$19,928.00	$73,873.93
Roast Beef & Swiss Sandwich	$4.39	810	17,550	210,600	5	60	$1,141.40	$7,365.56	$19,484.17	$72,228.63
Roast Beef Sandwich	$3.59	390	8,450	101,400	2	29	$933.40	$6,023.31	$15,933.53	$59,066.24
Steak & Cheese Sandwich	$3.89	550	11,917	143,000	3	41	$1,011.40	$6,526.65	$17,265.02	$64,002.14
Turkey Sandwich	$3.39	330	7,150	85,800	2	25	$881.40	$5,687.75	$15,045.86	$55,775.64

Item Name	Cost	Srv	Calories		Pounds		Yearly Cost	10% Interest Compounded Savings		
			Month	Year	Mth	Yr		5 Years	10 Years	20 Years
Bacon, Egg & Cheese Biscuit	$2.59	480	10,400	124,800	3	36	$673.40	$4,345.51	$11,495.22	$42,613.25
Breakfast Burrito	$1.99	550	11,917	143,000	3	41	$517.40	$3,338.83	$8,832.23	$32,741.45
Breakfast Quesadilla	$1.39	370	8,017	96,200	2	27	$361.40	$2,332.15	$6,169.25	$22,869.66
Cinnamon Bun	$0.87	260	5,633	67,600	2	19	$226.20	$1,459.69	$3,861.33	$14,314.10
Cinnamon Cake Stick	$0.69	450	9,750	117,000	3	33	$179.40	$1,157.68	$3,062.43	$11,352.56
Egg and English Muffin Sandwich	$1.99	290	6,283	75,400	2	22	$517.40	$3,338.83	$8,832.23	$32,741.45
French Toast Dips	$1.49	370	8,017	96,200	2	27	$387.40	$2,499.93	$6,613.08	$24,514.96
Ham, Egg & Cheese Bagel	$2.59	550	11,917	143,000	3	41	$673.40	$4,345.51	$11,495.22	$42,613.25
Hash Browns	$1.19	130	2,817	33,800	1	10	$309.40	$1,996.59	$5,281.59	$19,579.06
Pancakes	$2.49	600	13,000	156,000	4	45	$647.40	$4,177.73	$11,051.39	$40,967.95
Sausage and English Muffin Sandwich	$1.49	360	7,800	93,600	2	27	$387.40	$2,499.93	$6,613.08	$24,514.96
Sausage Biscuit	$1.69	410	8,883	106,600	3	30	$439.40	$2,835.49	$7,500.74	$27,805.56
Sausage Biscuit with Egg	$1.99	490	10,617	127,400	3	36	$517.40	$3,338.83	$8,832.23	$32,741.45
Sausage Breakfast Burrito	$1.39	290	6,283	75,400	2	22	$361.40	$2,332.15	$6,169.25	$22,869.66
Sausage, Egg & English Muffin Sandwich	$1.99	440	9,533	114,400	3	33	$517.40	$3,338.83	$8,832.23	$32,741.45
Scrambled Eggs	$2.49	180	3,900	46,800	1	13	$647.40	$4,177.73	$11,051.39	$40,967.95
BAGELS & CREAM CHEESE										
Blueberry Bagel	$0.69	330	7,150	85,800	2	25	$179.40	$1,157.68	$3,062.43	$11,352.56
Chive Cream Cheese	$1.30	100	2,167	26,000	1	7	$338.00	$2,181.14	$5,769.80	$21,388.89
Chocolate Chip Bagel	$0.69	310	6,717	80,600	2	23	$179.40	$1,157.68	$3,062.43	$11,352.56
Cinnamon Raisin Bagel	$0.69	320	6,933	83,200	2	24	$179.40	$1,157.68	$3,062.43	$11,352.56

Item Name	Cost	Calories			Pounds		Yearly Cost	10% Interest Compounded Savings		
		Srv	Month	Year	Mth	Yr		5 Years	10 Years	20 Years
Everything Bagel	$0.69	310	6,717	80,600	2	23	$179.40	$1,157.68	$3,062.43	$11,352.56
Garden Veggie Cream Cheese	$1.30	90	1,950	23,400	1	7	$338.00	$2,181.14	$5,769.80	$21,388.89
Honey Grain Bagel	$0.69	330	7,150	85,800	2	25	$179.40	$1,157.68	$3,062.43	$11,352.56
Onion Bagel	$0.69	310	6,717	80,600	2	23	$179.40	$1,157.68	$3,062.43	$11,352.56
Plain Bagel	$0.69	300	6,500	78,000	2	22	$179.40	$1,157.68	$3,062.43	$11,352.56
Plain Cream Cheese	$1.30	90	1,950	23,400	1	7	$338.00	$2,181.14	$5,769.80	$21,388.89
Poppy Bagel	$0.69	310	6,717	80,600	2	23	$179.40	$1,157.68	$3,062.43	$11,352.56
Pumpernickel Bagel	$0.69	320	6,933	83,200	2	24	$179.40	$1,157.68	$3,062.43	$11,352.56
Sesame Bagel	$0.69	320	6,933	83,200	2	24	$179.40	$1,157.68	$3,062.43	$11,352.56
Strawberry Cream Cheese (light)	$1.30	70	1,517	18,200	0	5	$338.00	$2,181.14	$5,769.80	$21,388.89
Sundried Tomato Bagel	$0.69	320	6,933	83,200	2	24	$179.40	$1,157.68	$3,062.43	$11,352.56

DONUTS

Item Name	Cost	Srv	Month	Year	Mth	Yr	Yearly Cost	5 Years	10 Years	20 Years
Bavarian Kreme Donut	$0.69	210	4,550	54,600	1	16	$179.40	$1,157.68	$3,062.43	$11,352.56
Chocolate Frosted Donut	$0.69	200	4,333	52,000	1	15	$179.40	$1,157.68	$3,062.43	$11,352.56
Chocolate Iced Glazed Donut	$0.87	280	6,067	72,800	2	21	$226.20	$1,459.69	$3,861.33	$14,314.10
Chocolate Kreme Filled Donut	$0.69	270	5,850	70,200	2	20	$179.40	$1,157.68	$3,062.43	$11,352.56
Glazed Cake Donut	$0.69	280	6,067	72,800	2	21	$179.40	$1,157.68	$3,062.43	$11,352.56
Glazed Cake Stick	$0.69	490	10,617	127,400	3	36	$179.40	$1,157.68	$3,062.43	$11,352.56
Glazed Chocolate Cake Stick	$0.69	470	10,183	122,200	3	35	$179.40	$1,157.68	$3,062.43	$11,352.56
Glazed Donut	$0.69	180	3,900	46,800	1	13	$179.40	$1,157.68	$3,062.43	$11,352.56
Glazed Twist Donut	$0.87	210	4,550	54,600	1	16	$226.20	$1,459.69	$3,861.33	$14,314.10

Item Name	Cost	Srv	Calories		Pounds		Yearly Cost	10% Interest Compounded Savings		
			Month	Year	Mth	Yr		5 Years	10 Years	20 Years
Jelly Filled Donut	$0.69	210	4,550	54,600	1	16	$179.40	$1,157.68	$3,062.43	$11,352.56
Jelly Stick	$0.69	530	11,483	137,800	3	39	$179.40	$1,157.68	$3,062.43	$11,352.56
Maple Frosted Donut	$0.69	210	4,550	54,600	1	16	$179.40	$1,157.68	$3,062.43	$11,352.56
Maple Iced Glazed Donut	$0.87	250	5,417	65,000	2	19	$226.20	$1,459.69	$3,861.33	$14,314.10
Old Fashioned Cake Donut	$0.69	300	6,500	78,000	2	22	$179.40	$1,157.68	$3,062.43	$11,352.56
Plain Cake Stick	$0.69	420	9,100	109,200	3	31	$179.40	$1,157.68	$3,062.43	$11,352.56
Powdered Cake Donut	$0.69	330	7,150	85,800	2	25	$179.40	$1,157.68	$3,062.43	$11,352.56
Sugar Donut	$0.87	200	4,333	52,000	1	15	$226.20	$1,459.69	$3,861.33	$14,314.10
Vanilla Iced Cake with Sprinkles Donut	$0.87	280	6,067	72,800	2	21	$226.20	$1,459.69	$3,861.33	$14,314.10

Sweet Indulgences

Item Name	Cost	Srv	Calories		Pounds		Yearly Cost	10% Interest Compounded Savings		
			Month	Year	Mth	Yr		5 Years	10 Years	20 Years
Banana Split	$2.89	510	11,050	132,600	3	38	$751.40	$4,848.85	$12,826.71	$47,549.15
Chocolate Chip Ice Cream	$1.59	270	5,850	70,200	2	20	$413.40	$2,667.71	$7,056.91	$26,160.26
Chocolate Cone (medium)	$1.39	340	7,367	88,400	2	25	$361.40	$2,332.15	$6,169.25	$22,869.66
Chocolate Cone (small)	$1.09	240	5,200	62,400	1	18	$283.40	$1,828.81	$4,837.76	$17,933.76
Chocolate Ice Cream	$1.59	270	5,850	70,200	2	20	$413.40	$2,667.71	$7,056.91	$26,160.26
Chocolate Malt (medium)	$2.49	880	19,067	228,800	5	65	$647.40	$4,177.73	$11,051.39	$40,967.95
Chocolate Malt (small)	$1.99	650	14,083	169,000	4	48	$517.40	$3,338.83	$8,832.23	$32,741.45
Chocolate Shake (medium)	$2.39	770	16,683	200,200	5	57	$621.40	$4,009.95	$10,607.56	$39,322.65

| Item Name | Cost | Calories | | | Pounds | | Yearly Cost | 10% Interest Compounded Savings | | |
		Srv	Month	Year	Mth	Yr		5 Years	10 Years	20 Years
Chocolate Shake (small)	$1.89	560	12,133	145,600	3	42	$491.40	$3,171.05	$8,388.40	$31,096.15
Chocolate Sundae (medium)	$1.99	400	8,667	104,000	2	30	$517.40	$3,338.83	$8,832.23	$32,741.45
Chocolate Sundae (small)	$1.69	280	6,067	72,800	2	21	$439.40	$2,835.49	$7,500.74	$27,805.56
Cinnamon Twists	$0.79	150	3,250	39,000	1	11	$205.40	$1,325.46	$3,506.26	$12,997.86
Dipped Cone (medium)	$1.59	490	10,617	127,400	3	36	$413.40	$2,667.71	$7,056.91	$26,160.26
Dipped Cone (small)	$1.39	340	7,367	88,400	2	25	$361.40	$2,332.15	$6,169.25	$22,869.66
Double Fudge Brownie	$2.39	360	7,800	93,600	2	27	$621.40	$4,009.95	$10,607.56	$39,322.65
Hot Carmel Sundae	$1.39	360	7,800	93,600	2	27	$361.40	$2,332.15	$6,169.25	$22,869.66
Hot Fudge Sundae	$1.39	340	7,367	88,400	2	25	$361.40	$2,332.15	$6,169.25	$22,869.66
Frosted Fudge Brownie	$2.39	440	9,533	114,400	3	33	$621.40	$4,009.95	$10,607.56	$39,322.65
Pralines 'n Cream Ice Cream	$1.59	280	6,067	72,800	2	21	$413.40	$2,667.71	$7,056.91	$26,160.26
Rainbow Sherbet	$1.59	160	3,467	41,600	1	12	$413.40	$2,667.71	$7,056.91	$26,160.26
Strawberry Shake (small)	$1.69	360	7,800	93,600	2	27	$439.40	$2,835.49	$7,500.74	$27,805.56
Strawberry Sundae (medium)	$1.99	340	7,367	88,400	2	25	$517.40	$3,338.83	$8,832.23	$32,741.45
Strawberry Sundae (small)	$1.69	240	5,200	62,400	1	18	$439.40	$2,835.49	$7,500.74	$27,805.56
Vanilla Cone (large)	$1.59	410	8,883	106,600	3	30	$413.40	$2,667.71	$7,056.91	$26,160.26
Vanilla Cone (medium)	$1.39	330	7,150	85,800	2	25	$361.40	$2,332.15	$6,169.25	$22,869.66
Vanilla Cone (small)	$1.09	230	4,983	59,800	1	17	$283.40	$1,828.81	$4,837.76	$17,933.76
Vanilla Ice Cream	$1.59	250	5,417	65,000	2	19	$413.40	$2,667.71	$7,056.91	$26,160.26
Vanilla Shake (medium)	$1.79	440	9,533	114,400	3	33	$465.40	$3,003.27	$7,944.57	$29,450.85

Item Name	Cost	Calories			Pounds		Yearly	10% Interest Compounded Savings		
		Srv	Month	Year	Mth	Yr	Cost	5 Years	10 Years	20 Years
Vanilla Shake (small)	$1.49	330	7,150	85,800	2	25	$387.40	$2,499.93	$6,613.08	$24,514.96
Walnut Fudge Brownie	$2.39	380	8,233	98,800	2	28	$621.40	$4,009.95	$10,607.56	$39,322.65
COOKIES										
Butter Toffee Cookie	$1.49	290	6,283	75,400	2	22	$387.40	$2,499.93	$6,613.08	$24,514.96
Cinnamon Sugar Cookie	$1.49	300	6,500	78,000	2	22	$387.40	$2,499.93	$6,613.08	$24,514.96
Milk Chocolate & Walnuts Cookie	$1.49	320	6,933	83,200	2	24	$387.40	$2,499.93	$6,613.08	$24,514.96
Milk Chocolate without Nuts Cookie	$1.49	280	6,067	72,800	2	21	$387.40	$2,499.93	$6,613.08	$24,514.96
Oatmeal, Raisins, and Walnuts Cookie	$1.49	280	6,067	72,800	2	21	$387.40	$2,499.93	$6,613.08	$24,514.96
Peanut Butter Cookie	$1.49	310	6,717	80,600	2	23	$387.40	$2,499.93	$6,613.08	$24,514.96
Semi-Sweet Chocolate Cookie	$1.49	280	6,067	72,800	2	21	$387.40	$2,499.93	$6,613.08	$24,514.96
Semi-Sweet Chocolate w/ Nuts Cookie	$1.49	310	6,717	80,600	2	23	$387.40	$2,499.93	$6,613.08	$24,514.96
White Chunk Macadamia Cookie	$1.49	310	6,717	80,600	2	23	$387.40	$2,499.93	$6,613.08	$24,514.96

Gourmet Drinks

Item Name	Cost	Calories			Pounds		Yearly	10% Interest Compounded Savings		
		Srv	Month	Year	Mth	Yr	Cost	5 Years	10 Years	20 Years
Café Latte	$3.05	260	5,633	67,600	2	19	$793.00	$5,117.30	$13,536.84	$50,181.62
Café Mocha w/ whip	$3.35	400	8,667	104,000	2	30	$871.00	$5,620.64	$14,868.33	$55,117.52
Café Mocha w/o whip	$3.35	300	6,500	78,000	2	22	$871.00	$5,620.64	$14,868.33	$55,117.52

| Item Name | Cost | Calories | | | Pounds | | Yearly Cost | 10% Interest Compounded Savings | | |
		Srv	Month	Year	Mth	Yr		5 Years	10 Years	20 Years
Cappuccino	$3.05	150	3,250	39,000	1	11	$793.00	$5,117.30	$13,536.84	$50,181.62
Caramel Blended Coffee Drink w/ whip	$3.55	430	9,317	111,800	3	32	$923.00	$5,956.20	$15,755.99	$58,408.12
Caramel Blended Coffee Drink w/o whip	$3.55	280	6,067	72,800	2	21	$923.00	$5,956.20	$15,755.99	$58,408.12
Coffee Blended Drink w/o whip	$3.15	260	5,633	67,600	2	19	$819.00	$5,285.08	$13,980.67	$51,826.92
Cranberry Smoothie	$3.85	420	9,100	109,200	3	31	$1,001.00	$6,459.54	$17,087.49	$63,344.02
Iced Café Latte	$3.05	160	3,467	41,600	1	12	$793.00	$5,117.30	$13,536.84	$50,181.62
Mango Smoothie	$3.85	500	10,833	130,000	3	37	$1,001.00	$6,459.54	$17,087.49	$63,344.02
Mocha Blended Drink w/ whip	$3.35	420	9,100	109,200	3	31	$871.00	$5,620.64	$14,868.33	$55,117.52
Mocha Blended Drink w/o whip	$3.35	290	6,283	75,400	2	22	$871.00	$5,620.64	$14,868.33	$55,117.52
Peach Smoothie	$3.85	460	9,967	119,600	3	34	$1,001.00	$6,459.54	$17,087.49	$63,344.02
Raspberry Smoothie	$3.85	480	10,400	124,800	3	36	$1,001.00	$6,459.54	$17,087.49	$63,344.02
Strawberry Smoothie	$3.85	450	9,750	117,000	3	33	$1,001.00	$6,459.54	$17,087.49	$63,344.02
Tazo Chai	$3.10	290	6,283	75,400	2	22	$806.00	$5,201.19	$13,758.75	$51,004.27

SAMPLE DAILY MONEY CALORIE COUNTER

Food Item	Cost	Calories
Blended Coffee Drink	$3.55	430
Glazed Donut	$0.69	180
Hamburger	$0.99	320
French Fries	$1.29	290
Total	$6.52	1,220

Yearly Amount (multiply total daily cost and calories by 260 days, which equates to 5 days per week) $1,695.20

Calories   317,200

Pounds (divide calories by 3,500 to get the amount of pounds)   91

DAILY MONEY CALORIE COUNTER

Food Item	Cost	Calories
Total		

Yearly Amount   _____
Calories   _____
Pounds   _____

Visit our Web site at www.richandthinliving.com to calculate the compound interest.

3

Other Addictions:
Silent Money Thieves

NOT EVERYONE INDULGES IN mochas and hamburgers on a regular basis. Maybe you are someone who eats healthily and never eats out. In fact, you prefer to eat rice cakes for lunch because you want to save money and calories. Good for you. But chances are, you have other purchase addictions, whether you know it or not. Meaning, there are certain purchases that you make regularly because it is just too hard to walk away. These types of addictions will not help you build personal wealth.

In fact, many of us have certain things that we just can't say no to. Over a long period of time, these purchases add up. In fact, you would be shocked to find out how much you are spending on these items every week, month, and year. If you purchase two compact disks a month, you are spending approximately $30 a month, not including tax. Over a one-year span, you will have spent $360 just on CDs. If you keep up this pattern for five years, you will have spent $1,800. That's a lot of money and a lost opportunity in terms of paying down your debt and boosting your assets. And speaking of debt, many people use their credit card to fund their addiction. A credit card feeds that impulse shopping habit. It's instant gratification, and everyone is affected by it at one point or another. Let's first take a look at common purchase addictions.

Books/Magazines. The idea of having a full bookshelf and more books and magazines than you could possibly read appeals to you. You love perusing magazines or books and reading up on your favorite topics. How many books or magazines have you bought this month? How much did you spend? Try visiting the library. You can check out videos and books and review magazines for free.

CDs. If you are spending a lot of money on music, consider listening more often to the radio—it's free. Another option is to buy used CDs at a fraction of the cost of new ones.

Cigarettes. This is a tough one. Cigarette smoking is a serious addiction, and one that's difficult to break. However, if you are able to kick the habit, think of all the money you'll be saving. At $4 per pack and one pack a day, you're spending $1,460 a year. What if you kicked the habit and put that amount of money aside in a mutual fund? You would have $9,421.51 in 5 years, $24,922.81 in 10 years, and $92,389.88 in 20 years!

Clothes. If buying clothes is your purchase addiction, chances are you already know that you are spending a lot of money. Buying just two items of clothing each month at the total price of $80 means you will have spent $960 in a single year. That's a lot of money, but it gets worse. If you invested $80 a month into a mutual fund instead, you would have banked over $16,000 in 10 years. Now, we understand that we all need clothes, so what if you cut back just half of the amount you're spending? In our example, that would equal $40 a month. If you put this amount into a mutual fund, you would have over $8,000 in 10 years.

Electronics. Are you a person who wants the newest and greatest electronic gizmo? Electronics often carry heavy price tags. Think about all the electronics you have purchased in the last year. How many of those items do you actually use? How much did you spend?

Facials. We all want to look young and have great skin. However, facials are costly. There are many facial products that you can buy and use at home. Purchasing these will save you a considerable amount of money.

Golf and golf equipment. Golf is a relaxing activity and a terrific social outlet. It is also an expensive hobby. What are you paying in green fees? How much do you spend on golf equipment? Stop to consider: Do the golf courses in your area have discounted green fees for certain days and times of the week? Are there any public courses on which you can play?

Hair care. For some people, personal hair care products are their purchase addictions. They purchase numerous different products—too many to actually use. We would guess that if many of us looked in our own bathroom cabinets, we'd find many bottles of unused shampoos, conditioners, hair sprays, and styling products.

Jewelry. When we say jewelry, we are including both fine and costume jewelry. Jewelry purchases tend to be costly. And, how many rings, watches, and earrings could you possibly need? Do you really need a necklace in every color?

Makeup. Most women would confess that they have either a box, drawer, or bag filled with makeup that they don't use. It's a fact: makeup purchases are an addiction for many women, and often those purchases are made as an impulse, especially if a "free gift" is offered based on a minimum purchase. The department stores know how to entice you with these offers. How many items in the free gift do you really use? We have drawers full of free samples that have just collected dust.

Manicures and pedicures. These are some of life's luxuries, having your hands and feet massaged and polished. They are relaxing activities—but also expensive, especially when you consider the length of time the polish remains without chipping. Cut back on the amount of times per month that you visit the nail salon.

Massages. While massages are relaxing and a very nice indulgence, the $45 to $100 you are spending can be put to another use. Being debt-free would also be relaxing, wouldn't it?

Movies. If you are a movie buff, chances are you love going to the theater. Prices of movies at the box office are increasing. With tickets costing anywhere from $6 to $9 and up, a night out at the movies turns into an expensive affair. Imagine the money you would save if you made it a habit to go to matinee movies instead or, even better, to rent movies.

Purses. Look in your closet. How many purses do you see? There may be purses in there that you have barely used or never worn at all. If so, purses could be your purchase addiction.

Sales. If you go to a sale and make purchases just because the products are on sale, you have an addiction. You end up with things that you don't need because you can't resist buying something (anything) on sale.

Shoes. Sandals, boots, loafers, tennis shoes, daytime, evening, casual, dressy—there are so many types of shoes from which to choose. Yet, even if you are buying your shoes at discount stores, if you are constantly buying them, you're forfeiting money that could be put to another use. Do you even wear all those shoes? If you have more shoes than you do clothes, shoe shopping is probably your addiction. How many pairs of black shoes do you really need?

Software programs. Computers are a huge part of our society, and it seems that there is a software program for just about everything. Do you have numerous software programs that you have purchased and don't use? Are you buying software on a regular basis just because it looks interesting?

Sports events. So many of us love sports: hockey, soccer, football, baseball, basketball, and so on. However, tickets to sports events are not cheap. If this is your purchase addiction, consider buying cheaper seats, or, if possible, watch the game for free on your television or listen to it on the radio.

Video games. The prices of video games can be anywhere from $5 to $50. Put that money in savings or toward paying off your debt.

Your purchase addiction may not have been listed here, but the key is to think about what you habitually spend your money on: it could be auto accessories, home improvement, or picture frames (believe it or not, this is one of our purchase addictions). Take a moment and reflect on those purchases that you just can't say no to and list them in the worksheet on the next page.

My Purchase Addictions

Item	# Purchased per month	Price per item	Cost each month
Shoes	2	$40.00	$80.00

Were you surprised to see how much you are spending each month on these addictions? Think about your wish list in Chapter 1, "Everyone's Money Dream." What were some of your wishes? If one of them was to have no more credit card debt, the insight gleaned from the above exercise can help you keep from creating additional debt and even start to pay it down, as noted in the example below.

Your Credit Cards

(The following example assumes an interest rate of 21% APR and a minimum payment of 4%).

Creditor	Balance	Minimum Payment
ABC Bank	$1,000.00	$40.00
XYZ Creditor	$500.00	$20.00
Favorite Department Store	$250.00	$10.00

Assuming you are already allocating $70 per month for the minimum payments, you now can put an additional $80 per month toward your debt by eliminating shoe purchases. In this example, we are paying the lowest balances first, as you will see. Once a credit card is paid off, we allocate the money from monthly payments to the next credit card. Here is what you would do:

Month One

Creditor	Balance	Monthly Payment
ABC Bank	$1,000.00	$40.00
XYZ Creditor	$500.00	$20.00
Favorite Department Store	$250.00	$90.00
	Total	**$150.00**

Month Two

Creditor	Balance	Monthly Payment
ABC Bank	$960.00	$40.00
XYZ Creditor	$480.00	$20.00
Favorite Department Store	$160.00	$90.00
	Total	**$150.00**

Month Three

Creditor	Balance	Monthly Payment
ABC Bank	$920.00	$40.00
XYZ Creditor	$460.00	$40.00
Favorite Department Store	$70.00	$70.00
	Total	**$150.00**

Creditor	Balance	Monthly Payment
ABC Bank	$880.00	$40.00
XYZ Creditor	$420.00	$110.00
Favorite Department Store	$0	$0
	Total	**$150.00**

These examples do not take into account interest charges per month. It is a simple example to show you how you can allocate your money to accomplish a financial goal of getting out of debt. It may appear that we are telling you to deprive yourself of the things you most enjoy. That's not the case. We're trying to show you how you can cut back in certain areas so you can make the desires on your wish list come true. Refer to Chapter 10, "Mmm... A Taste for Luxury," to see how you can still enjoy your favorite things.

The following credit card table shows you the effect of making extra payments on your credit balances.

Credit Card Chart

Balance	# Months Until Paid	Total Interest Paid	$5 Extra		$10 Extra	
			Interest Saved	Saved # Months	Interest Saved	Saved # Months
$2,000	193 (16.1 yrs)	$2,504.62	$738.59	70 (5.8 yrs)	$1,113.70	101 (8.4 yrs)
1,900	189	$2,364.62	$714.91	69	$1,073.24	100
1,800	185	$2,224.65	$690.21	69	$1,031.26	99
1,700	180	$2,084.61	$664.31	67	$987.56	97
1,600	176	$1,944.63	$637.15	67	$942.14	96
1,500	171	$1,804.61	$608.60	66	$894.78	94
1,400	165	$1,664.65	$578.54	65	$845.32	92
1,300	159	$1,524.64	$546.71	63	$793.55	90

Balance	# Months Until Paid	Total Interest Paid	$5 Extra		$10 Extra	
			Interest Saved	Saved # Months	Interest Saved	Saved # Months
1,200	153	$1,384.64	$512.96	62	$739.26	87
1,100	146	$1,244.65	$477.06	60	$682.17	85
1,000	138	$1,104.63	$438.66	58	$621.96	81

GREG'S ADDICTION

Greg had been frustrated over the years because he felt that he was not saving for retirement at the rate he would like. Plus, he had some credit card debt that he just couldn't seem to pay off. There never seemed to be enough money left after paying his bills for retirement or to get out of debt. In counseling Greg about his situation, we asked him to list his daily expenditures. He believed that he wasn't spending a lot on food and beverages each day. In fact, he wasn't a coffee drinker, and he usually brought his lunch from home so he wouldn't have to go out while he was at work. However, once Greg started reflecting on his spending behavior, he made a confession. Apparently, Greg liked to think of himself as someone who kept up with technology: a person who always has the cutting-edge electronics and computer equipment. Every year Greg purchased a new personal digital assistant (PDA) because he wanted to have a PDA with up-to-date technology, even though he didn't necessarily need a new device. Greg determined that he was spending on average $500 each year on a PDA.

Over a five-year span, Greg spent $2,500! That realization didn't sit well with Greg. He had personal financial goals that he wanted to accomplish—getting out of debt and saving for retirement—and new PDAs were eating up a chunk of his money. He decided to cut back on his PDA purchases. Instead of purchasing a new device each year, he decided to upgrade every other year. Greg put the money he was saving toward his financial goals and is well on his way to building his personal wealth.

Is shopping in general your addiction? Take this short quiz:

YOU KNOW YOU ARE A SPENDAHOLIC WHEN ...

Answer: True or False

1. The clerk greets you by name. _____
2. Products are put aside just for you in your favorite color and size. _____
3. You know the date and time of every sale. _____
4. You put the store address as your home address on an application by mistake. _____
5. Every time your spouse calls you on your mobile phone, you happen to be in the same store. _____
6. If you can't make up your mind between two items, you purchase both. _____
7. Just thinking about shopping makes your heart start racing and your palms start sweating. _____

8. You sneak the new shoes you purchased into the house because you don't want your spouse to know.
_____

9. You spend all your extra time shopping. _____

If you had one or more True answers, you are a spendaholic. Refer to the section below, "Great Solutions for the Spendaholic."

GREAT SOLUTIONS FOR THE SPENDAHOLIC

1. When the products are set aside for you, politely reply, "No thank you, but thank you for thinking of me."

2. If you know the date and time of every sale, make sure to make other plans for those dates and times.

3. If you can't make up your mind on a purchase, go home and don't buy either one.

4. If your heart starts beating fast and your palms get sweaty when thinking about shopping, take some deep breaths.

5. If you sneak shoes into the house, stop buying shoes.

6. Spend your extra time on a fun hobby, or some exercise, which will keep your figure in shape!

SAMPLE NON-FOOD ADDICTION WORKSHEET

Item	Cost	Purchase Frequency	Cost per Month (costs multiplied by purchase frequency)	Cost per Year (cost per month multiplied by 12 months)
Music CDs	$15.00	2/mo.	$30.00	$360.00
Sports Events	$25.00	1/mo.	$25.00	$300.00
Total			**$55.00**	**$660.00**

NON-FOOD ADDICTION WORKSHEET

Item	Cost	Purchase Frequency	Cost per Month (costs multiplied by purchase frequency)	Cost per Year (cost per month multiplied by 12 months)
Total				

4

Saving Money and Calories

CUTTING BACK ON BOTH YOUR food and your purchase addictions is a great way to build personal wealth, but there are other ways to fatten up your savings account and pay off debt. Did you know that the average household carries over $10,000 in credit card debt? Our financial reckoning day comes when our debt is greater than our income, and what causes such a sad occurrence is losing control of where our money goes. Don't fall victim to this trap; take control by getting a grip on your spending.

JOHN AND MARY'S STORY

John and Mary felt like they were on a sinking ship. For years they had gotten into the habit of borrowing money from family members or taking cash advances from their credit cards because their bills were so high. They would run short of money at the end of every month. There never seemed to be enough money. It was easy to tap into their home equity line of credit until that too was maxed out. Bankruptcy seemed like an option, but they knew they wanted to try to pay off the credit card companies as well as debt owed to family members.

Before our appointment, we instructed John and Mary to list all their bills, including living expenses and income, for us to review together. As we reviewed the list, we could see all the bills that they wrote down plus their living expenses. If you looked at their calculations, their income seemed enough; however, there were missing entries. When we questioned John and Mary about their miscellaneous expenses, such as eating out, fast food, clothing allowances, and so on, neither one of them had a clue as to how much they were spending. That was the root of their problems: not accounting for the incidental expenses.

The first thing we instructed them to do was to both get a journal or notepad. Then we instructed them to evaluate, for the next 30 days on a daily basis, every penny that they spent, listing the items the money was going toward. At the end of the 30 days, each item was to be put in a specific category. With the totals from each of the categories, it would be apparent where their excess money was going.

John and Mary were shocked to see how much they were spending each week eating out and going to their favorite coffee houses. By reducing these outings, they were able to save over $250 per month and apply that toward their debt.

Where is your money going each month? To figure this one out, make a list of *every* penny you spend for at least 30 to 60 days. And we mean *every* penny. For example, if you purchase a 50-cent soda from the vending machine, write it down! If you're married, both you and your spouse must track every penny you spend and write it down. Don't forget to track your credit card purchases too.

Create categories for your spending. Be specific! Don't write down "miscellaneous" as an entry. The goal is to determine exactly where your money is going, so "miscellaneous" won't cut it. Write down what the item was that you purchased and how much you spent. And include the date of the purchase on your list.

One thing people miss categorizing properly is their ATM withdrawals and debit card purchases. These must be broken down. If you get $20 from your ATM, separately list every penny you spend that cash on. The ATM withdrawal is the number-one problem for letting money slip through your fingers. You know the feeling: you look in your wallet, and that $20 you withdrew the day before is gone and you don't know where it went! You're not alone. Most people, if asked, haven't a clue as to where their money goes. If you're being charged a fee for using your ATM, write that down as well.

By keeping a journal and recording the cash you spend for various categories, you are better able to save that money and apply it instead toward your bills and savings. We can recommend several ways you can save money to reduce your debt as well as fatten your savings account. It's like dieting: it may be painful at first, but if you do it long enough, it will become a habit and then a way of life. Once you have formed the habit of spending wisely, you will think twice before you make the purchase.

Let's take a look at an example from the Money Calorie Counter to give you an idea of how you can cut spending (along with calories).

Hamburger & French Fries

Put the same amount aside that you would be spending on hamburgers and french fries and increase your savings by $722.80 a year. You will also have saved yourself 70 extra pounds during the year!

CASH AND CREDIT CARD JOURNAL WORKSHEETS

Examples of the different categories would be meals, fast food, sodas, coffee, clothing, prescriptions, toiletries, gasoline, magazines, and books. List other categories, if applicable. Remember, every penny must be listed. Here's an example of a typical Daily Cash Expenditures worksheet, as well as one you can use for your own calculations.

Sample Daily Cash Expenditures Worksheet

Item	Amount
ATM	$0.00
Meals	$12.00
Drinks	$3.00
Clothing	$0.00
Toiletries	$0.00
Books	$0.00
Entertainment	$8.00
Other:	$0.00
Total	**$23.00**

Daily Cash Expenditures Worksheet

Item	Amount
ATM	
Meals	
Drinks	
Clothing	
Toiletries	
Books	
Entertainment	
Other:	
Total	

Here's an example of a typical One-Week Cash Expenditures worksheet, as well as one you can use for your calculations.

Sample One-Week Cash Expenditures Worksheet

Date	ATM	Meals	Drinks	Clothing	Toiletries	Books	Entertainment
Sunday		$25.00		$20.00			
Monday		$12.00	$3.00				$ 8.00
Tuesday						$10.00	
Wednesday		$ 7.00	$3.50				
Thursday					$22.00		
Friday							
Saturday	$20.00						$16.00
Total	**$20.00**	**$44.00**	**$6.50**	**$20.00**	**$22.00**	**$10.00**	**$24.00**

One-Week Cash Expenditures Worksheet

Date	ATM	Meals	Drinks	Clothing	Toiletries	Books	Entertainment
Sunday							
Monday							
Tuesday							
Wednesday							
Thursday							
Friday							
Saturday							
Total							

Here's an example of a typical 30-Day Cash Expenditures worksheet, as well as one you can use for your own calculations.

Sample 30-Day Cash Expenditures Worksheet

Date	ATM	Meals	Drinks	Clothing	Toiletries	Books	Entertainment
9/1	20.00		3.23				
9/2		25.31					14.00
9/3		7.50			5.99		
9/4		33.38		57.76			
9/5	40.00		5.87				
9/6							
9/7					18.94		
9/8		14.77	2.50				
9/9						12.80	
9/10		6.74					
9/11			1.00				
9/12		13.75					10.76
9/13					31.22		
9/14		5.75	3.25				
9/15							24.00
9/16	20.00		2.75				
9/17				25.53	10.76		
9/18		17.03	1.75				
9/19							
9/20		9.95			6.63		
9/21			3.25				
9/22		7.95					8.45
9/23	20.00						
9/24		5.56	1.50				
9/25				39.16			
9/26			1.00				
9/27		23.00					
9/28					3.55	8.93	
9/29		4.54	1.50				
9/30							14.00
Total	**100.00**	**175.23**	**27.60**	**122.45**	**77.09**	**21.73**	**71.21**

30-Day Cash Expenditures Worksheet

Date	ATM	Meals	Drinks	Clothing	Toiletries	Books	Entertainment
Total							

Here's an example of a 30-day Credit Card Expenditures worksheet, as well as one you can use for your own calculations. For your own worksheet, be sure to list any categories you need to, including one other than the ones shown in the example, if applicable. Remember, every penny must be listed. Save receipts to compare with your statement.

Sample 30-Day Credit Card Expenditures Worksheet

Date	Merchant	Meals	Fast Food	Clothing	Gasoline	Other
9/1	Mama's Pizza	22.19				
9/5	Marty			42.53		
9/8	Uno				15.00	
9/14	Pete's Burger		5.66			
9/16	Clothes, Inc.			24.89		
9/21	Tool Depot					129.04
9/23	Book.com					35.55
9/29	ABCStation				18.25	
Total		**22.19**	**5.66**	**67.42**	**33.25**	**164.59**

30-Day Credit Card Expenditures Worksheet

Date	Merchant	Meals	Fast Food	Clothing	Gasoline	Other
Total						

Just by tracking your daily cash and credit expenditures, you will find ways to cut back on spending and apply that money to pay bills and beef up your savings. Think how much money you can save if you commit to a daily spending journal *and* the Money Calorie Counter! Especially if your money is going toward calorie consumption.

MONEY-SAVING TIPS

Here is a list of different money-saving tips:

Automobile Expenses

- Buy a used car instead of a new car. You will save quite a bit of money.
- Pump your own gas rather than go to the full-service island.

Banking

- Review your business and personal checking account bank statements. Total the monthly service charges, plus all the additional charges you are accumulating each time you make ATM withdrawals (outside your bank's network) and/or debit card transactions that incur fees from the merchants. That can amount to an additional 20-plus dollars per month.
- To eliminate these charges, find a bank that doesn't charge monthly service fees.
- Go only to the ATM machines that are affiliated with your bank, and that don't charge fees. This can save you $1 to $2 per transaction.

- Dump your change daily into a box, bottle, or container. It adds up quickly.

Credit Cards

- Review your credit card statements every month. You would be surprised at the amount of errors. There may be charges you never made listed on the statement or finance charges you should not have incurred. Compare your monthly statement to the worksheet of your previous charges and receipts.
- Pay your credit card balances off in full each month and eliminate the finance charges and interest from ongoing balances.

Electricity, Gas, Water

- Change the thermostat by 1 degree. By adjusting your thermostat 1 degree, you will save a significant amount of money on your next bill.
- Cut down on your water use. Don't let the faucet run while you brush your teeth. Take shorter showers.

Entertainment

- Quit buying lottery tickets. You will be a winner by depositing the money into a mutual fund instead.
- Cut out a cable channel you don't watch. Eliminate extra channels and stick to the basic plan. If possible, cut out cable altogether.
- Rent videos instead of going out to the movies.

- Check out movies and books from the library. Why pay to rent movies when you can have free access to them?
- Go to matinees instead of evening movies.

Insurance

- Review your car insurance policy. Shop around for cheaper rates. Get higher deductibles.

Meals and Beverages

- Bring your own soft drink instead of buying one from a vending machine. You could save $0.60 to $1.00 or more if you do. Bringing your own would cost you only $0.25. How many do you drink per day? And…what about the calories?
- Go to a fancy coffee house and you will pay approximately $3 per cup or more. Calculated on five workdays per week, that will total $15 per week, which is $780 per year. Think about how many cans of coffee you could have purchased at the grocery store and how much home-brewed coffee you could have taken with you in a thermos. With the amount you spend at your favorite coffee house each year, you could pay off one large, looming bill. Brew your own at home.
- Every time you have the urge to eat out—don't! Be sensible when deciding whether or not to go out for a meal. Take the money you would have spent and put it in a fund for money saved. Apply that money to a bill.

- When eating out, split dinners. Order water instead of drinks. Put the money into your fund for money saved.
- When you're debt-free, you can really celebrate. Until then, every penny counts.

Memberships and Subscriptions

- Drop your gym and health club membership. Invest in video workouts. Don't buy expensive exercise equipment. Use a cinderblock or a step stool to do your step aerobics and canned vegetables for weights.
- Get your news from the Internet, radio, or television instead of the newspaper.
- Don't renew your magazine subscriptions. Save money by reading free articles on the Internet. Many of the very same print magazines you pay for post their feature articles online for free viewing.

Shopping

- Avoid impulse purchases. When you are out shopping for clothes, or a major purchase, go home and think about it. Sleep on it. Oftentimes doing so will eliminate an impulse purchase.
- Comparison shop. If there is an item you absolutely need to buy, check out the prices at other stores before you make the purchase.
- Take advantage of rebates. If you buy a product that comes with a rebate offer, use it. Even if the amount seems low, money from rebates will add up quickly.

- Shop at garage sales and secondhand stores for clothes and toys. Go to discount stores to get your best buys.

Groceries

- Clip coupons and shop at grocery stores that will double or even triple your coupon's value.
- You've heard it before: never grocery shop when you are hungry! And for good reason. There's a greater chance that you will buy groceries you don't need and spend extra money when you are hungry.

Telephone

- Shop long-distance carriers. You will be amazed how just 1 cent per minute difference in plans can add up.
- Lower your cell phone bill. If you don't have unlimited calling (which is expensive), resist the urge to chat, and use your cellular phone only for emergencies.
- Cancel call waiting, three-way calling, and caller ID from your telephone.
- Don't use the IM or email function on your cell phone if you are not certain that these features are a part of your plan.

Put the money you save from applying these tactics into a special account designed to pay off debt and begin saving for the future. Here's an example of what happened to coauthor Melinda and her husband, as told in her own words.

MIKE AND MELINDA'S STORY

Several years ago Mike had a drop in income due to a change in his job. We knew that money was going to be tight when he switched careers, but we had no idea that it was going to be as tight as it ended up being.

It was initially hard for us to change our spending. We were used to a certain lifestyle and it was very difficult to change. I had to examine our budget (which I must admit I hadn't created until we were in our financial crisis). The amount of money we were spending on eating out was too high, and we started to cut back. I made meals at home, and we split dinners when we went out with friends. It was very difficult in the beginning, but after a while it became easier, as we were able to use the money we were saving to pay all of our bills. During that time in our lives, not one bill was unpaid.

Once we got over the hump, we definitely became more aware of our spending, not only then, but currently. We always think twice to see where we can cut back and save money.

Complete the following worksheet. When you have completed all the worksheets in this chapter, compare the worksheets with one another and see how much money you have saved.

Extra Cash Worksheet Example

Create a list of things you can do to save money and apply it toward your bills or savings. Enter the date, the item you saved money on, and the amount you saved. Don't forget to set the savings aside to put into a special fund. Do this daily.

Date	Item	Cost	Amount Saved
9/14	Soda		0.35
9/14	Coffee		1.75
9/14	Meal		9.00
		Total Savings	11.10

Extra Cash Worksheet

Date	Item	Cost	Amount Saved
		Total Savings	

5

Budget versus Calories

UP TO THIS POINT, YOU HAVE
learned how to find hidden money, cut back on spending,
and even save extra calories. Now it's time to dive into
budgets. Making a budget might not be the most exciting
or eagerly anticipated thing to do. But setting one up is
crucial, as it is an essential tool for creating personal
wealth. When you want to lose weight, you write down
the amount of calories and portions you can have. The
same holds true when you are setting up a budget. You
need a guide to follow.

Many people fall into the debt trap by either not having a budget or having one and not sticking with it. Once
you get a handle on your finances, budgeting and staying
with it will become automatic. Don't believe anyone who
tells you that you don't need to follow a budget. Of
course, you can do your own thing and not follow an offi-

cial, written-in-stone budget. But if you're going to do it that way, you still need to know what is coming in and what is going out. And, don't forget, initially you need to have everything written down to master your financial plan. Wealthy people have a direction and roadmap for how they are going to make money work for them (the key here is that wealthy people make money work for them, not the opposite). Our recommendation is that you develop a budget and let it become a way of life for you by referring to it often to ensure you are headed in the right direction.

Let's be honest—setting up and committing to a budget is not easy. It's no surprise that the effort involved can be just like what you put in when starting a diet. In the beginning, the undertaking is time consuming and often frustrating. You may even feel deprived. Sticking with a budget takes discipline and accountability. However, as with a good diet, the eventual benefits are extremely rewarding. Remember your wish list from Chapter 1? Having and following a budget will help you turn those wishes into reality.

SETTING UP YOUR BUDGET

When setting up a budget, be honest with yourself: list *all* the debts that you have. Just as cheating on a diet doesn't help you, neither does cheating on your budget. Locate your previous month's bills to use as a reference. Be sure to include your everyday living expenses, such as bagels and lattes (you may even want to list the calories). If you used the 30-day expenditure journal we described in the previous chapter, you can use that as a guide here. Also, include your credit card purchases too.

Most people fail to include fast food and coffee stops in their budget. Refer to the Money Calorie Counter for a money checkup.

Next, calculate how much money you have coming in each month to pay your bills. If your spouse earns income, include that in your figures. Child support, alimony, and any other income should also be figured in.

With your expenses and income calculated, you can now set your monthly budget. A monthly budget will help you stay focused on the whole picture and see how much money you need to bring in to pay all your bills. It will also show you why you are short each month and why your debt doesn't change much. Lastly, it can help you determine what amount you need to set aside each month to achieve some of the items on your wish list.

If you find that your expenses are higher than your income, you can use the Money Calorie Counter to help you determine where to cut back on your spending. Apply those savings toward helping with your expenses.

Setting a yearly budget would definitely be helpful if you are self-employed or paid on commission, since you don't know from month to month how much you will be making.

WARNING!

If you are self-employed or just earning commission, don't just spend the large amount of money you earn in a given month. This type of spending gives you a false sense of security. You don't really make that amount each and every month; undoubtedly, your income will fluctuate. If you spend all your money during one month when you're flush, you may come up short the following month, when your income is relatively low. You need to determine what it takes *per year* for you and your household to pay your bills. Go back and review your bank and credit card statements. Then divide that number by 12. The amount you calculate should be set aside every month, regardless of whether it's a good or bad one. In fact, if you're flush one month, try and stay ahead by two or three months. Doing so will eliminate catch-up time when another month is slow.

Here are some percentages that make up a typical budget. These percentages are in relation to your overall budget amount.

Housing	20–30%
Utilities	4–7%
Food	15–20%
Transportation	6–20%
Medical	2–8%
Clothing	2–4%
Investment/Savings	5–10%
Debt Payments	10–15%
Tithing/Charitable Giving	5–10%
Misc.	5–10%

For example, let's say your overall budgeted expenses equal $3,800. Here's how your budget would look:

Expense	Amount	Percent
Housing	$1,064	28%
Utilities	$190	5%
Food	$684	18%
Transportation	$380	10%
Medical	$152	4%
Clothing	$114	3%
Investment/Savings	$266	7%
Debt Payments	$380	10%
Tithing	$380	10%
Misc.	$190	5%
Total	$3,800	100%

BUDGET BUSTERS

You need to plan ahead for expenditures that have to be paid once a year, quarterly, or monthly; these costs must be added into the monthly budget. We call these *Budget Busters*. Most people forget to add these costs into their monthly budget, and so they come up short when the bill is due.

Examples of common Budget Busters are property taxes, home insurance, and car maintenance. You need to make projections for such nonmonthly expenses in your budget. For example, suppose your yearly property tax bill is $1,200. You would divide the $1,200 total by 12 (the number of months in one year). This would give you $100—the amount you would need to set aside each month so the bill could be paid when due. These expenses would be then added to the monthly budget.

Having these items listed in the Budget Buster categories will force you to save for these expenses, so you won't be left short when the bill comes due. If necessary, a separate mutual fund or money market account should be opened to hold this money so you aren't tempted to spend it.

CALCULATING YOUR NET WORTH

One of the first things you should do before creating your budget and gaining control of your finances is to calculate what your *net worth* is. If you were to apply for a business loan, home loan, or automobile loan, you would complete an application that would give the potential lender an idea of what your net worth is. Your net worth is calculated by taking your total assets and subtracting your total liabilities. You should determine what your net worth is at the beginning of every year, to see what progress you are making in accomplishing your goals.

By knowing what your net worth is, you will be able to see your wealth grow.

A few years ago, coauthor Deborah counseled a couple who was facing financial difficulties. Their story has stood out in Deborah's mind. The following is her recounting of their situation.

MARK AND JENNY'S STORY

Mark and Jenny were rapidly losing ground with their finances. Jenny worked part-time, and Mark had a job in sales where he was paid strictly by commission.

There was no consistency from year to year; during some years, Mark's annual income was quite high. During others, his income dropped off. The problem with Mark and Jenny was that they were living as though every year was the same, meaning as if Mark's income was always on the high side (it wasn't). They were spending money recklessly. If you asked them where their money went, neither one knew. They had become accustomed to a certain lifestyle and were unwilling to change. The unfortunate thing was they had no more chances. They were spending more than they had coming in. Reckoning day had arrived.

Every month they were unable to pay their bills. Mark had even cashed in his pension and 401(k). He was now using cash advances from his credit cards to pay bills. They were maxed out on the cards and drowning in debt.

After we carefully reviewed their debts, it was apparent that they were a step away from bankruptcy. They had three children living at home, all in private schools, with one about to start college. If they didn't make drastic changes, there would be severe financial consequences.

The list of debts they had prepared wasn't the whole picture. There was no breakdown of all the miscellaneous expenses or annual expenses listed, which painted a false picture.

The first thing I advised them to do was to make a journal and write down every dollar they spent for the next 60 days. I told them to meet with me at the end of 30 days and categorize each purchase and total the amounts spent. I instructed them to continue this procedure another 30 days to see where their money was going. This would give them a full 60 days to review and determine where they could cut back.

Since Mark was paid on commission, both Mark and Jenny needed to prepare an annual budget to see on how much money they needed to live. The annual budget would help them prepare their monthly budget.

When the total annual budget was completed, Mark and Jenny could calculate exactly how much they needed to set aside each month. If Mark received a high commission check for one month that was over and above what they needed, he was to set aside that money to add to the following month's commission. It was important that they stay two to three months ahead of their bills, setting money aside to save them from being short when the commissions were low.

By setting a monthly budget, and eliminating excess expenditures (the "fast food" of their budgets), Mark and Jenny were able to figure out exactly where their money was being spent. It was a slow process to get their budget under control, but they were eventually able to put aside the money they needed each month and live within their means.

SETTING MONEY ASIDE

It is important that you always strive to have at least three to six months of living expenses saved: three months saved if you are married and both working; six months, if you are single or a one-income household. If you do that, then if your income drops or an emergency occurs, you will have enough money set aside to take care of you and your household.

To get that money in hand, you need to use the Money Calorie Counter. Please refer to Chapter 2, "Money Calorie Counter," and add up the amount of money you can save by avoiding certain purchases. Use this money to build your rainy-day fund and invest for your future. If you were able to save $167 a month, that would equate to over $2,000 in a year.

The following is an example from the Money Calorie Counter of what you can save by not buying lattes:

Café Latte

Item Name	Cost	Calories			Pounds		Yearly Cost	10% Interest Compounded Savings		
		Srv	Month	Year	Mth	Yr		5 Years	10 Years	20 Years
Café Latte	$3.05	260	5,633	67,600	2	19	$793.00	$5,117.30	$13,536.84	$50,181.62

If you were to cut out your daily latte and put that money into your savings account, you would have $793 in a year, plus avoiding putting on 19 pounds. The idea is to save even more money than that, so refer to the Money Calorie Counter and Chapter 3, "Other Addictions" to see if you can cut back on any other indulgences. To be "money savvy," you need to have a money cushion and know what comes in as well as what goes out.

Sample Net Worth Statement

Assets:	
Cash on Hand	$ 125.00
Checking Account	653.00
Savings Account	4,978.00
Money Markets	5,000.00
Stocks & Bonds	15,000.00
Cash Value Life Insurance	25,000.00
Automobiles (Value)	22,700.00
Real Estate (Value)	250,000.00
Household Goods	9,700.00
Total Assets	**$333,156.00**
Liabilities:	
Real Estate Loan	$150,000.00
Automobile Loan	15,000.00
Student Loan	14,000.00
Credit Card Balances	9,890.00
Department Stores	764.00
Medical Expenses	1,000.00
Total Liabilities	**$190,654.00**
Total Assets minus Total Liabilities = $142,502.00 Net Worth	

Net Worth Statement

Assets:

Cash on Hand _____

Checking Account _____

Savings Account _____

Money Markets _____

Accounts Receivable _____

Stocks & Bonds _____

Notes Receivable _____

Cash Value Life Insurance _____

Automobiles (Value) _____

Real Estate (Value) _____

Household Goods _____

Business _____

Inventory _____

Other Assets _____

Total Assets _____

Liabilities:

Real Estate Loan _____

Automobile Loan _____

Student Loan _____

Credit Card Balances _____

Department Stores _____

Accounts Payable _____

Taxes Payable _____

Medical Expenses _____

Other Liabilities _____

Total Liabilities _____

Total Assets minus Total Liabilities = _____ **Net Worth**

BUDGET BUSTERS

The following are examples of Budget Busters (non-monthly expenses).

Housing:
>   Property taxes
>   Home insurance
>   Security systems
>   Home repairs/maintenance (yard)
>   Maintenance agreements

Utilities:
>   Waste management
>   Water/water softener

Automobiles:
>   Automobile insurance
>   Auto registrations (all vehicles)
>   Auto maintenance and repairs

Medical:
>   Medical insurance
>   Life insurance
>   Disability insurance
>   Doctor/dental
>   Orthodontia
>   Vision exam/contacts/glasses
>   Health maintenance

Memberships and subscriptions:
>   Church tithing
>   Organizations/clubs
>   Professional licenses
>   Sports

Warehouse clubs

Magazines

Schooling:

School tuition

Books/supplies

Office:

Office equipment maintenance

Clothing:

Work clothes

School uniforms

Clothes, adult and children

Sport clothes

Recreation:

Recreational hobbies

Vacations

Music lessons

Pets:

Pet maintenance

Training

Miscellaneous:

Accountant

Taxes

Savings

Investments

Gifts (birthday, anniversary, etc.)

Holidays

Other

If you're not sure how much you are spending, flip through the past year's check register and credit card statements. Also refer to your cash and credit card journals mentioned in Chapter 4, "Saving Money and Calories." Look through the Money Calorie Counter to find those items in which you indulge; add the amounts you spent for those items to your budget.

When you do this, you will know exactly how much you spend and where the money goes.

Budget Buster Worksheets

Check the list of Budget Busters above and determine which items you buy or are obligated to pay throughout the year. If there are other items not listed on these worksheets that you purchase at some point during the year, add them to your budget. Be sure to allocate costs on a monthly basis.

To do that, determine the total yearly cost for all items that are nonregular expenses and divide that amount by 12. This amount is what you need to set aside each month in a special fund to pay for the individual items when due. It also is the total that you would enter on your personal monthly budget worksheet.

Take this same approach for business expenses and business budgets, if you have a business.

Sample Nonmonthly Expenses Worksheet

Category	Item	Yearly Estimates
Housing	Property Tax	$1,400.00
Automobiles	Auto Repair	800.00
Schooling	Books	515.00
Miscellaneous	Savings	200.00
Pets	Training	150.00
Total = $3,065.00	$3,065.00/12 months = $255.42	

Nonmonthly Expenses Worksheet

Category	Item	Yearly Estimates

Sample Personal Monthly Budget Worksheet

Income	
Salaries	$3,400.00
Wages (if self-employed)	
Commissions	
Dividends	
Rental Income	500.00
Other	
TOTAL INCOME	$3,900.00
Fixed Expenses	
Mortgage/Rent/Housing	$1,125.00
Savings	300.00
Automobile Payments	350.00
Automobile Insurance	140.00
Medical and Dental Care	75.00
Education	
Internet	18.95
Cable	
Other	
Total Fixed Expenses	$2,008.95
Variable Expenses	
Utilities	250.00
Groceries	300.00
Telephone	75.00
Tithing/Giving	400.00
Taxes	
Other (take from nonmonthly list)	255.42
Total Variable Expenses	$1,280.42
Installments	
Credit Cards	255.00
Credit Line	

Other	
Total Installments	$255.00
Occasional Expenses	
Clothing	100.00
Recreation	50.00
Other	
Total Occasional Expenses	150.00
TOTAL EXPENSES	**$3,694.37**
TOTAL INCOME MINUS EXPENSES	**$205.63**

Personal Monthly Budget Worksheet

Income	
Salaries	
Wages (if self-employed)	
Commissions	
Dividends	
Rental Income	
Other	
TOTAL INCOME	
Fixed Expenses	
Mortgage/Rent/Housing	
Savings	
Automobile Payments	
Automobile Insurance	
Medical and Dental Care	
Education	
Internet	
Cable	
Other	
Total Fixed Expenses	

Variable Expenses	
Utilities	_____
Groceries	_____
Telephone	_____
Tithing/Giving	_____
Taxes	_____
Other (take from nonmonthly list)	_____
Total Variable Expenses	_____
Installments	
Credit Cards	_____
Credit Line	_____
Other	_____
Total Installments	_____
Occasional Expenses	
Clothing	_____
Recreation	_____
Other	_____
Total Occasional Expenses	_____
TOTAL EXPENSES	_____
TOTAL INCOME MINUS EXPENSES	_____

Sample Yearly Budget Worksheet

Income	
Salaries	$40,800.00
Wages (if self-employed)	_____
Commissions	_____
Dividends	_____
Rental Income	6,000.00
Other	_____
TOTAL INCOME	$46,800.00

Fixed Expenses

Mortgage/Rent/Housing	13,500.00
Savings	3,600.00
Automobile Payments	4,200.00
Automobile Insurance	1,680.00
Medical and Dental Care	900.00
Education	
Internet	227.40
Cable	
Other	
Total Fixed Expenses	**$24,107.40**
Variable Expenses	
Utilities	3,000.00
Groceries	3,600.00
Telephone	900.00
Tithing/Giving	4,800.00
Taxes	
Other (take from nonmonthly list)	3,065.00
Total Variable Expenses	**$15,365.00**
Installments	
Credit Cards	3,060.00
Credit Line	
Other	
Total Installments	**$3,060.00**
Occasional Expenses	
Clothing	1,200.00
Recreation	600.00
Other	
Total Occasional Expenses	**$1,800.00**
TOTAL EXPENSES	**$44,332.40**
TOTAL INCOME MINUS EXPENSES	**$ 2,467.60**

Yearly Budget Worksheet

Income

Salaries

Wages (if self-employed) _____

Commissions _____

Dividends _____

Rental Income _____

Other _____

TOTAL INCOME _____

Fixed Expenses

Mortgage/Rent/Housing _____

Savings _____

Automobile Payments _____

Automobile Insurance _____

Medical and Dental Care _____

Education _____

Internet _____

Cable _____

Other _____

Total Fixed Expenses _____

Variable Expenses

Utilities _____

Groceries _____

Telephone _____

Tithing/Giving _____

Taxes _____

Other (take from nonmonthly list) _____

Total Variable Expenses _____

Installments

Credit Cards _____

Credit Line _____

Other	_____
Total Installments	_____
Occasional Expenses	
Clothing	_____
Recreation	_____
Other	_____
Total Occasional Expenses	_____
TOTAL EXPENSES	_____
TOTAL INCOME MINUS EXPENSES	_____

6

Keep More Money and
Shrink Your Debt

YOU'VE WORKED ON SHRINKING
your calories—now it's time to work on reducing your
debt with the money you saved by using the Money
Calorie Counter (as well as the other addictions you've
avoided spending on). Getting out of debt is serious business. It takes discipline and perseverance. In order to
build wealth, you don't want to be bogged down with
excessive debt. There are several different strategies to
accomplish getting out of debt. You need to see which one
fits your situation, and apply it. It's like dieting: not every
diet works for you.

Do you have any idea how much your present balance, credit limit, payment, and interest rate is on all your
credit cards? Complete the following Debt worksheet.
Don't look! Try it first without looking at your statements. Now, once you have completed it, let's do a reality

check. Complete a second Debt worksheet listing all the accounts and information from your recent credit card statements. How knowledgeable were you? Compare the two worksheets by totaling your balances and payments. Keep the second Debt worksheet (with your credit card statement information) close by because you will be using it as a reference point for getting out of debt.

DEBT WORKSHEET #1

From Your Memory

No Peeking!

List each creditor's name, the balance owed to that creditor, and that creditor's credit limit, minimum payment, and interest rate.

_____

_____

_____

_____

_____

_____

_____

_____

_____

_____

_____

_____

_____

_____

_____

DEBT WORKSHEET #2

From Your Credit Card Statements

List each creditor's name, the balance owed to that creditor, and that creditor's credit limit, minimum payment, and interest rate.

_____

_____

_____

_____

_____

_____

_____

_____

_____

_____

_____

_____

_____

_____

_____

Are you surprised by the differences you see between worksheet 1 and worksheet 2?

Most individuals know very little about the details on their credit cards because they don't read the credit card statements each month. Generally, people will just look at the payment due and perhaps the balance on each statement, but that is all. In fact, the majority of credit card users are more aware of what their payment is than what interest rate they are paying. By not knowing what you are paying in interest, you will prolong the life of the debt. That is especially so if you are making only the minimum monthly payment.

To shrink debt, the first thing you must do is stop using credit cards altogether. It would make no sense trying to pay off old debt while accumulating new debt. And, you can't build wealth by paying high interest rates on your current credit cards or loans. You are only throwing your money away. It's like dieting; excessive calories add more pounds. High-interest credit cards add years to your debt.

Once you have reviewed your Debt Worksheet 2, you may consider moving amounts currently on the major credit cards with high interest rates to the lower-interest-rate cards. For example, let's say you have two credit cards. One has a credit limit of $4,000, an interest rate of 16 percent, and a balance of $1,200. Your other credit card has a credit limit of $2,000, an interest rate of 21 percent, and a balance of $1,800. Transfer the $1,800 amount from the credit card with the 21 percent interest rate to the credit card with the 16 percent interest rate (provided transfers are offered and the interest rate on transfers is 16 percent or less). You would now owe $3,000 on the credit card with the 16 percent interest rate. You have saved 5 percent interest. You will now be able to pay off the total $3,000 debt more rapidly because you're saving money on interest. The key in making this work is that you *don't charge anything else to the high-interest-rate account.* To play it safe, stop using the card—destroy it if need be—but keep the account open for some time afterwards. This will help you build your credit score.

Department store credit cards should be consolidated to one of your lower-interest-rate credit cards. Interest rates on department store cards are usually higher than those on most credit cards, and range from 21 percent to higher amounts. Stop using the account after you transfer the balance.

The average household carries a minimum of five credit cards with balances. Oddly enough, most of us never calculate how long it will take to pay off any of that credit card debt, nor how much we actually will pay in interest payments before the debt is paid off. Let's do so now.

Say that you have a card with a balance of $2,000. If you made no new charges to the card and simply paid the minimum payment, it would take over 16 years to pay off the credit card! The interest paid would be $2,504.62, plus the $2,000 principal, which would mean you paid $4,504.62 in total for using your charge card.

By adding an extra payment—$5, $10, or more—to your monthly credit card payment, you would help yourself to pay off your debt more quickly, and you'd save a large amount in interest charges.

Look at the sample credit card chart in Chapter 3, "Other Addictions: Silent Money Thieves," and see how much you'd save by adding more money to your payments, above and beyond your minimum payment. Spending is like consuming calories: the more we take in, the larger we get. Conversely, the more we save, the lighter we get.

If you are not sure where to get the extra money to pay off your debt, review the Money Calorie Counter. It will give you many ideas of ways to save and cut calories. Here are two examples:

Tazo Chai Gourmet Drinks

| Item Name | Cost | Srv | Calories | | Pounds | | Yearly Cost | 10% Interest Compounded Savings | | |
			Month	Year	Mth	Yr		5 Years	10 Years	20 Years
Tazo Chai	$3.10	290	6,283	75,400	2	22	$806.00	$5,201.19	$13,758.75	$51,004.27

If instead of purchasing those Tazo Chai drinks five days a week at $3.10 per drink, you put the money toward your debt, you would be paying down an additional $806 per year. And you'd also be saving 75,400 calories in a year!

| Item Name | Cost | Srv | Calories | | Pounds | | Yearly Cost | 10% Interest Compounded Savings | | |
			Month	Year	Mth	Yr		5 Years	10 Years	20 Years
Raspberry Smoothie	$3.85	480	10,400	124,800	3	36	$1,001.00	$6,459.54	$17,087.49	$63,344.02

At the end of the year, write a check to your credit card company in the amount of $1,000, because that's the amount you will have saved for the 12 months if you forgo those raspberry smoothies. You will also avoid 124,800 calories that year and a possible 36 pounds.

PAYING OFF YOUR CREDIT CARDS

After you have reviewed your Debt worksheet, prioritize each credit card from the highest credit card balance to the lowest credit card balance.

For example:

Company	Balance
ABC Company	$2,300.00
XYZ Company	1,200.00
ALPHA Credit Card	1,000.00
Department Store A	500.00
Department Store B	275.00

Experts have different opinions about which to pay off first: high interest, high balances, or high interest with low balances. The decision is yours, but the quickest way to get out of debt and feel like you are accomplishing something is to pay off the lower balances first. The payment you would be making to the lowest balance now that it's paid off should be added to the next credit card balance you are trying to pay off. For instance, for the Department Store B balance of $275, you have been making a monthly payment of $10. Once this full balance is paid off, add the $10 you were paying to Department Store B to the minimum payment ($10) for the next highest balance of $500, for Department Store A; continue making the $20 payment ($10 + $10) until this second card also is paid off. Then take the two payments you were making on the cards for the two department stores, totaling $20, and add it to the $20 minimum payment you have been making to the next highest balance card (the ALPHA Credit Card, balance $1,000). These extra payments you apply to the principal on the various cards will cause the balances to decrease rapidly.

A SIMPLE CALL

Another way to lower your monthly payments is to call your credit card company and request it to lower your interest rate. Many times companies will, but we have found they won't automatically reduce your interest rate. You must call to request it.

CREDIT CARD PAYMENT WORKSHEETS

Use the worksheet below to calculate how quickly you will be able to pay off your credit card debt. We have provided an example of a typical worksheet, using the credit card balance figures above. Your list should include the month, creditor name, balance, minimum payment and the amount you paid. In this example, you are allocating $500 per month toward credit card payments. Use the $500 allocated amount to add to payments even after you pay off each creditor. Once you pay off your last creditor, take the monthly savings of $500 and put it in a mutual fund or interest-bearing account monthly to add to your wealth.

Sample Payoff Strategy Worksheet

Based on an allocated amount of $500.00 per month.

Month	Creditor	Balance, $	Minimum Payment, $	Amount Paid, $
Month 1				
	ABC Company	2,300.00	40.00	45.00
	XYZ Company	1,200.00	19.00	25.00
	ALPHA Credit	1,000.00	20.00	25.00
	Dept. Store A	500.00	10.00	130.00
	Dept. Store B	275.00	10.00	275.00
Month 2				
	ABC Company	2,255.00	40.00	45.00
	XYZ Company	1,175.00	19.00	25.00
	ALPHA Credit	975.00	20.00	60.00
	Dept. Store A	370.00	10.00	370.00
	Dept. Store B	0	0	0
Month 3				
	ABC Company	2,210.00	40.00	45.00
	XYZ Company	1,150.00	19.00	25.00

Month	Creditor	Balance, $	Minimum Payment, $	Amount Paid, $
	ALPHA Credit	915.00	15.00	430.00
	Dept. Store A	0	0	0
	Dept. Store B	0	0	0

Payoff Strategy Worksheet

Month	Creditor	Balance, $	Minimum Payment, $	Amount Paid, $

NOT REDUCING YOUR
YEARLY ESTIMATED PAYMENTS

At the beginning of each year, when you are doing your projected expenses (see the Yearly Budget worksheet in Chapter 5, "Budget versus Calories"), and you have estimated a certain amount to be paid toward credit card debt, divide that amount by 12 (months). As you begin to pay down the debt and your balances decrease, your minimum payments will decrease. Use the amount that you estimated to pay monthly toward principal to continue paying the balances down. Don't gauge the amount that you need to pay by the minimum amount shown on your statement.

For example, if you have calculated from your yearly worksheet that $6,000 per year will be paid toward credit card debt, divide that amount by 12 months. This equals $500 per month that you will pay toward credit card bills. Since the balances are decreasing and the minimum payments are being reduced, you need to stick with your plan and continue to budget $500 per month and apply the excess to whatever credit card you want to pay off first. Don't look at excess money as extra until all your debts are paid off. Then, when everything is paid off, take that excess money and add it to your savings account or mutual fund each month.

EQUITY LOANS AND REFINANCING

Refinancing your mortgage is an option only if the payment is lower than you are paying now. The refinance could be for a lower interest rate or to consolidate your bills. If it is to consolidate your bills, then your monthly mortgage payment must be lower than the bills you are paying off and the mortgage payment added together. For example, if your mortgage is $1,000 per month and you have credit card bills totaling $500 per month, that would total $1,500. If your total payment after refinancing is $1,200, you will have saved $300. A lender will evaluate your situation by calculating the ratio of your monthly income to your new payment minus your debts. The ideal ratio is between 25 and 33 percent; with this ratio, you will probably qualify for the new loan. However, some lenders will go as high as 50 percent.

If it looks like your bills will be paid off within a three-year period without refinancing the house, don't do it. Refinancing should be done only if you are going to come out with a lesser payment, and if you are willing to discipline yourself by breaking the bondage of credit card use.

A refinance can cost thousands of dollars in loan fees and charges, plus you are extending the life of your loan. New mortgages could be for 15, 20, or 30 years.

A home equity loan is known as a second mortgage. It could be set up as a fixed rate for 15, 20, or 25 years, or set up as an equity line where you are approved for a certain amount of money (equity from your home) and you withdraw the money as you need it. For example, you may have an equity line of $50,000. You may only need to withdraw $15,000 for improvements, or to pay off credit cards. You can use the money however you want. The equity line works like a credit card. It also has the danger of being perceived as easy money. An equity line without a fixed interest rate or set number of years should not be your first choice, because the initial low interest rate can create a false sense of security and the interest rate can be racheted upward at a later time. The interest rate is usually lower for the first three months of the equity line and then will adjust to a much higher interest rate, which will make the payments higher than most people anticipate.

Be forewarned! If you become late on making the payments with a home equity loan, you risk losing your home through foreclosure, just as you would with your primary mortgage. Keep that point in mind.

When you refinance your property or try to obtain a second mortgage, there must be some equity in the property. If you are looking to refinance your whole loan, in order for you to get cash out, most lenders want to see a 75 to 80 percent or lower loan-to-value ratio. That means that if your property has an appraisal of $100,000, the lender will give you a loan of up to $75,000 or $80,000, depending on the lender. Let's say that your loan is for $75,000. To determine how much you would net, subtract the current balance of your mortgage from $75,000. For example, if the balance is $50,000 and you can borrow $75,000, you'll net $25,000 less the cost of your loan.

Some lenders will make 100 percent and 125 percent equity loans. You'll find it harder to qualify for these types of loans. The risk of getting a 100 percent or 125 percent loan is that you are overencumbering your property. You're taking all the equity out of your property...and then some. These types of loans are risky because if your property value drops, you will owe more than what the property is worth. It will make it difficult to sell your property.

MORTGAGE REDUCTION

You can reduce the life of your mortgage by adding additional money to your mortgage payment each month. For example, by setting up a biweekly payment schedule, you will reduce years off your loan. The biweekly payment equates to one extra mortgage payment a year. By paying one extra payment or more per year, you will save hundreds of thousands of dollars for the life of your loan.

Once your credit cards are paid off, add extra payments to your mortgage payment. If you add extra payments, make sure you write a note to your lender to apply the extra amount to the principal of your loan; you can generally note this on your monthly mortgage payment stub.

Visit our Web site at www.richandthinliving.com to find out how to calculate the savings on your loan by paying it biweekly.

CREDIT COUNSELORS AND DEBT MANAGEMENT

You should consider contacting a credit counseling company to consolidate your debt whether you are delinquent in your payments, are overextended with your credit cards, or are tired of paying high interest rates.

One question you may have is, will your credit report be tarnished if you use the services of a credit counseling company (or debt management company)? Credit counseling companies or debt management companies don't report your account to the credit reporting agencies. The creditors are the ones who may report to the credit reporting agencies that you are using a credit counseling company. It is up to a potential creditor viewing your report to determine whether that would impact their decision to issue you credit. Remember, if you are late or overextended on your accounts, your credit report is already tarnished. Getting help is your best solution.

Credit counselors are noted for their ability to rebuild your relationship with your creditors. They function as the middle party in communicating with your creditors, helping you to work out your problems and develop a repayment program that will satisfy both you and your creditors.

Most credit counseling companies offer a nonprofit service. A small monthly donation and small percentage (called the *fair share*) is paid to the company by the creditor.

When you contact a credit counselor, have a list of your bills ready, with the creditors' names, balances owed, and payments due. Also have at hand information regarding your income and living expenses. The counselor will look at your income, assets, debt, and expenses to determine what you can afford to pay.

If you have received any late notices, demand notices for payment, collection notices, legal suits, court judgments, or anything that you feel is significant for the counselor to review, have it ready to give to them. The counselor needs to see your whole financial picture in order to develop a payment plan that will help you and satisfy the creditors.

After receiving all the required information from you regarding your financial situation, the counselor will contact your creditors to work out a repayment schedule. The credit counseling company will set your payments so that you are making one monthly payment to the counseling service to cover all your debts. The counseling service will then disburse the payments to the creditors. You will know every month how much you will be spending toward your bills and be relieved to know that the balances are going down.

Most creditors are willing and able to work with a credit counseling service, because they recognize that you are seeking help and not filing for bankruptcy. They know that if you file for bankruptcy, it will be difficult, if not impossible, for them to be able to collect the debt.

The credit counselor will work with the creditors to lower the payment by reducing the interest to anywhere from 0 percent to 11 percent. (Each creditor will have a different formula used to lower the rate.) With the reduction in your interest rate, the payments that you will make regularly will drop below what you are paying now. The payments will apply more toward your principal than toward interest, which will allow you to pay off your debts in three to six years. By doing so, you will save thousands of dollars in interest overall and eventually be entirely debt free. Usually you will also stop accruing late fees and over-the-limit fees when you work with a credit counseling company. If you are late, the account will be re-aged, meaning it will be brought to a current status.

The debt management company we recommend is Cambridge Credit Counseling Corp. You can contact them at www.cambridgecredit.org or 800-226-2743; a link can also be found on one of our Web sites at www.financial victory.com. Don't wait until you are very deeply in trouble to seek help with your finances. It's never too late to get assistance. If you suspect you are overextended; are anticipating a job layoff, a divorce, or disability that would affect your financial situation detrimentally; or are experiencing a reduction of income, get some help right away.

SAVINGS ACCOUNTS

A question we often hear is: should I use my savings account to pay off my debts?

Look at it this way: if the money you have in savings is earning 6 percent interest and you are paying 18 percent or higher in interest on your debts, you're losing money. Keep a small amount of money in your savings account for a rainy day, but use the remaining money to pay down some of your debt.

BANKRUPTCY

Before ever considering a bankruptcy, make sure you have consulted a credit counseling or debt management company such as Cambridge Credit Counseling. This could be your bridge to help you to avoid a bankruptcy.

Bankruptcy laws have changed in recent years. It's not as easy as it used to be to eradicate a debt. Chapter 7 is much more difficult to get in discharging your debts. In most cases, a Chapter 13 will be required, where you make payments to the creditors based on court approval.

Be sure of what you are getting into, and contact an attorney. Filing for bankruptcy should always be the last resort. A bankruptcy will follow you for 10 years on your credit report. That could affect you detrimentally. For example, if an employer is considering hiring you and runs a credit report that mentions the bankruptcy, you may not get the job.

If you do file for bankruptcy, you will find that it takes several years for you to rebuild your credit report. During that time, when you apply for a mortgage, credit card, or automobile loan, you will be charged high interest rates.

Nevertheless, for some people, filing for bankruptcy is the right thing to do. You need to ask yourself, "Can I live with the consequences?" Don't file for a bankruptcy just because you are tired of hearing from the creditors. Don't let any creditor bully you into a bankruptcy. Contact a bankruptcy attorney to see if you are a candidate.

BORROWING FROM A
FAMILY MEMBER OR FRIEND

Sometimes a family member or friend will volunteer to help you financially. This option is not always the best one, as so many relationships are ruined because of money. If you do borrow money from someone close to you, sign a promissory note in which you agree to pay the loaner back when you have the funds. Don't use the money that you borrow from a family member or friend to pay credit card bills. Use it for survival. Such fundamental expenses would include rent or mortgage, food, and utilities. If you use the money for other things, you run the risk of falling behind with your rent or mortgage, not being able to feed your family, or having your utilities turned off.

Don't get into the bad habit of accepting money from family or friends. There has to come a point where you need to find other remedies to solve your financial problems. Don't use family or friends as a crutch.

Let's examine a situation in which a couple were having trouble making their debt payments and see how they approached the problem and what course of action they chose to get themselves out of it.

JAMES AND LISA'S STORY

James and Lisa had fallen behind in making their debt payments. Not all their payments were behind, but they knew that they were overextended and treading water. If any emergency were to happen, they would go under. Their interest rates were high on all their credit cards. It felt as if they would never be able to pay the debts off.

Bankruptcy seemed to be the only solution. James and Lisa came to see us, and they brought all their bills with a list of all their income and expenses. Their credit card payments were amounting to $700 per month, which was on top of all their other living expenses.

After reviewing their situation, we recommended that they contact a credit counseling company before filing for a bankruptcy. James and Lisa contacted a debt management firm, which was able to get them on the right debt management program. They were able to negotiate and get the creditors to reduce their interest rates and payments. Their credit card payments were reduced from $700 to $500 per month, and they were able to pay off the debts in less time.

When James and Lisa were able to see their payments reduced and that they would have their debts paid off within the four- to six-year period, they decided against filing for bankruptcy. They knew that in the long run their credit rating would appear better without having the stigma of a bankruptcy following them for the next 10 years.

If bankruptcy is your only option, remember that there have been many wealthy people who have filed for bankruptcy and been able to rebound from the experience to make new wealth. Just look at the stories of Mark Twain and Walt Disney—both of whom at one time had to file for bankruptcy! That didn't stop them from being ultimately successful.

PART TWO

Gain Wealth, Not Weight

7

Grow Your Money, Not Your Waistline

MOST PEOPLE DON'T KNOW the basics about how to increase their wealth, do financial planning, or save for their future, let alone being able to define the many financial terms and types of accounts that are out there. Frankly, most of the information goes over everyone's head. We all just want to have simple definitions to help make the best decisions.

In this chapter we will help you better understand the different functions of the basic accounts you hear and read about. Many credit unions and lending institutions offer financial advisors as well as services by Certified Financial Planners who can help you with the decisions you need to make regarding your accounts. There are financial advisors who can help you with a financial plan. It is important that you understand the different options you may have and what these financial terms mean.

COMPOUND INTEREST

If you are in your twenties, you have the time to see the power of compounding. For example, if you start saving $2,000 a year ($166.66 per month) at age 25 and keep it up until you reach age 35, and never add another penny to the account from then on, you'd have $682,881.84 saved by the time you reached age 65, based on 10 percent annual return. The growth comes from the interest and principal being compounded.

To get the same amount at age 65 if you started saving at age 45, you'd need to save $10,700 a year ($891.67 per month). So if you're currently in your forties or fifties, you need to make up for lost time. Start saving as much as possible by putting money into tax-deferred savings plans and other accounts. It's never too late to start saving, so take action now.

Check out the Compound Savings Chart to see how quickly the money can accrue if you start saving early.

Compound Savings Chart, at 10% return, compounded annually

Savings Time Period	Annual Savings Amount					
	$500.00	$1,000.00	$1,500.00	$2,000.00	$2,500.00	$3,000.00
5 years	$3,052.55	$6,105.10	$9,157.65	$12,210.20	$15,262.75	$18,315.30
10 years	$7,968.71	$15,937.42	$23,906.14	$31,874.85	$39,843.56	$47,812.27
15 years	$15,886.24	$31,772.48	$47,658.72	$63,544.96	$79,431.20	$95,317.45
20 years	$28,637.50	$57,275.00	$85,912.50	$114,550.00	$143,187.50	$171,825.00
25 years	$49,173.53	$98,347.06	$147,520.59	$196,694.12	$245,867.65	$295,041.18
30 years	$82,247.01	$164,494.02	$246,741.03	$328,988.05	$411,235.06	$493,482.07
35 years	$135,512.18	$271,024.37	$406,536.55	$542,048.74	$677,560.92	$813,073.11
40 years	$221,296.28	$442,592.56	$663,888.83	$885,185.11	$1,106,481.39	$1,327,777.67

You may be thinking to yourself: how can I find the money to put into savings? Refer back to Chapter 2, "Money Calorie Counter," and Chapter 3, "Other Addictions: Silent Money Thieves," to find ways to save money on expenses. Let's look at an example from the Money Calorie Counter.

Charbroiled BBQ Chicken Sandwich

		Calories		Pounds		Yearly	10% Interest Compounded Savings		
Item Name	Cost	Srv	Month	Year	Mth	Yr	Cost	5 Years	10 Years	20 Years
Charbroiled BBQ Chicken Sandwich	$2.99	290	6,283	75,400	2	22	$777.40	$5,016.63	$13,270.54	$49,194.44

Take the amount you would have spent on charbroiled BBQ chicken sandwiches and invest it in a mutual fund. In 5 years you could have $5,016.63 saved; in 10 years you could have $13,270.54 saved; in 20 years, $49,194.44.

Let's examine some types of financial products that will help you to achieve the types of savings you want while compounding your interest steadily.

TRADITIONAL SAVINGS PRODUCTS FROM BANKS AND LENDING INSTITUTIONS

These are the most common types of products available from a bank or credit union that will help you achieve a healthy savings over time. Which one is right for you will depend on your specific financial situation and goals. It is wise to always consult a financial advisor or Certified Financial Planner.

Certificate of Deposit (CD)

A certificate of deposit, or CD, is a deposit at your credit union or lending institution that has a guaranteed rate of interest for a specific period of time (for example, three months, one year, or three years). It differs from a savings deposit in that you are subject to a penalty if you withdraw the money early. All CDs are insured by the Federal Deposit Insurance Corporation (FDIC); deposit amounts are guaranteed up to $100,000 for a single account and $200,000 for a joint account.

Money Market Account (MMA)

A money market account, or MMA, is sponsored by a credit union or bank. You have access to your money in this account whenever you need it without incurring any penalties for withdrawal. The interest rates will fluctuate according to the current interest rates.

Talk to an advisor at your bank or credit union to see what type of MMA is best for your situation.

RETIREMENT ACCOUNTS

There's a lot to consider when planning for your retirement. In addition to figuring out what your own needs will be, you need to determine ways to allocate your money so that it builds income efficiently and wisely... and continues to grow and earn income after you have stopped working. There are a number of retirement accounts in which you can invest, which we will discuss below. All of these provide a means to do tax-advantaged investing. Essentially, "tax-advantaged" refers to accounts that

- Don't require you to pay taxes until you withdraw the money (known as *tax-deferred programs*)
- Allow you to lower your income taxes (known as *pretax programs*)

Before signing up for an account, you'll need to do a bit of research and crunch some numbers to see which programs are the best for you and your needs.

Individual Retirement Accounts (IRAs)

Individual retirement accounts, commonly known as IRAs, offer tax-deferred savings and sometimes tax-deductible contributions as well, depending on the type of account.

The one requirement for opening up an IRA is that you must have earned income—money paid to you for work services you performed. Additionally, you can only contribute a maximum amount annually so long as you don't contribute more than you earn. Since the maximum amount is subject to change, check with the person who prepares your taxes or your financial advisor for the amount you may contribute.

There are a number of different types of IRAs:

- Traditional deductible IRA
- Traditional nondeductible IRA
- SEP-IRA
- Roth IRA

The two traditional IRAs and the SEP-IRA are tax deferred, meaning that you will owe no tax until you withdraw your money. Basically, with a traditional tax-deductible IRA, you are able to take immediate advantage of tax savings once you contribute. Your account earnings are also tax deferred. However, should you need to withdraw from this account, you will need to pay taxes. In some instances, you may make a withdrawal without penalty due to a hardship such as a medical emergency, college tuition, or payment related to your home.

The traditional nondeductible IRA offers tax-deferred account earnings. Contributions to this account, however, are not tax deductible, and you will be required to pay taxes at regular rates when you withdraw except for the situations mentioned above.

The Simplified Employee Pension IRA, or SEP-IRA, is for the self-employed person or small business. You can make annual deposits to this account that are higher than the annual amounts you can pay to other types of IRAs. These contributions are tax deductible, and the money also grows tax deferred.

The Roth IRA is similar to the traditional IRA except that withdrawals are not required and the annual contribution is not tax deductible. Otherwise, they are tax free, meaning that your money can accumulate without you owing taxes on the earnings, even when you choose to withdraw, so long as you follow all the withdrawal rules for this type of account. Because you pay taxes on contributions up front, withdrawals of those contributions at any time are tax free. To qualify for tax-free withdrawal of accumulated earnings, your account must be opened for at least five years and you must be age 59½ (with exceptions for withdrawals mentioned above).

Separate Spousal Accounts

If one spouse works while the other stays home, you are eligible to contribute money to a separate account for the nonworking spouse. The benefit is that the stay-at-home spouse can build an individual retirement fund. Doing so is a terrific opportunity for married couples—one definitely worth taking advantage of.

To determine how much you need to accrue for the spouse, you'll need to use a retirement calculator. Calculate different scenarios, to see which one is appropriate. There are a number of such calculators available online, for example:

- www.about.com/money (check out the Personal Finance link)
- www.financialmuse.com
- www.moneycentral.msn.com/retire/home.asp

Take advantage of these sites to assist you with your retirement planning.

Opening Up an IRA

Opening an individual retirement account is easy: select a bank, brokerage firm, mutual fund company, or another financial institution with which you want to work. Apply for an IRA by completing the application form it provides. The institution you select will be referred to as the "custodian" or the "trustee" of your retirement account.

Be aware: individual retirement accounts are self-directed, meaning that you are responsible for deciding how the money is to be invested. You will also have to adhere to account rules as specified in the guidelines. Annual investments also need to be guideline approved. All contributions need to be reported to the Internal Revenue Service (IRS). If your contributions are tax deductible, you can take the deduction on your federal tax return. Otherwise, you'll need to fill out a Form 8606 for non-tax-deductible contributions.

IRA Investments

As IRAs are self-directed, you will have to figure out how you want your contributions directed: do you want the money invested in regular savings accounts? stocks and bonds? mutual funds? Per federal guidelines, you are not able to invest in certain things:

- Collectibles
- Fine art
- Gems
- Non-U.S. coins

Account guidelines also provide that you can buy and sell investments without paying taxes on any gains you may incur.

When Can I Make an IRA Contribution?

If you'd like to make an IRA contribution for the previous tax year, you need to open up the account by April 15. You can take advantage of spreading out your IRA deposit over a 15-month time period by having a standard amount deducted from your checking account and deposited into your IRA as of January 2. Chances are you won't feel the financial pinch as much as you would by opting to make a lump-sum deposit closer to the April 15 deadline. If you know that you're not a disciplined saver, choose to spread out your contributions. That way, you'll be building your retirement income steadily, and you will be less likely to put off your contribution.

401(k) and 403(b) Plans

Both 401(k) and 403(b) plans are retirement programs offered through your employer. The 401(k) plans are offered by companies, and 403(b) plans are offered by nonprofit organizations like charitable organizations, universities, and some hospitals. These plans allow you to defer taxes on a portion of your salary by electing to make an authorized contribution to your employer's program.

Contributions are typically a percentage of your paycheck. If the amount is deducted through a paycheck reduction, the contribution is considered pretax. The federal government has specific limits as to how much you can contribute to your plan. Most employers will allow you to contribute up to the limit.

Your contribution earnings will grow tax deferred. Taxes will not be assessed until you withdraw the money for retirement. Keep in mind that these plans are tax *deferred* and not tax *free*. Additionally, the amount of money you contribute is not reported on your W-2 form, which reduces your income and may affect your tax bracket.

To apply for a savings account, check with your employer. If your company offers a plan, then you'll need to sign off on an election form. This form authorizes the paycheck deductions that will be your plan contribution. You will also need to decide whether you want to select different investments or opt for investor packages determined by your employer.

Additional Benefits of the 401(k) and 403(b)

Some employers offer "company match" programs. This means that for every employee dollar, the employer matches the contribution with additional money, generally a predetermined percentage. This is a wonderful opportunity to enhance your retirement dollars. You're already contributing your own money, but to have additional money provided is just like getting free money!

Sometimes employers also allow you to take out loans based on your 401(k) plan. Loan repayments must be made on a regular basis and are usually figured at market rates. In this instance, you are not taxed on the money, nor is the loan considered a withdrawal. In some instances, as with IRAs, you may make a withdrawal due to a hardship such as a medical emergency, college tuition, or payment related to your home. Otherwise, should you withdraw from your 401(k) plan when you are younger than age 59½, you will have to pay penalties for early withdrawal. You may also forfeit the right to make contributions to your account for a set amount of time.

Differences Between IRAs and
401(k) or 403(b) Plans

If it's possible, you may want to take advantage of both types of retirement programs. However, if your budget only allows you to contribute so much, then you'll need to decide between the two. In brief, the features associated with an IRA are

- Lower contribution limit
- Nearly limitless investment opportunity
- May not significantly reduce your annual income for tax purposes

With a savings plan such as a 401(k) or 403(b), the options are

- Higher contribution limits
- Company match contributions (if this is part of the company program)
- May significantly reduce your annual income for tax purposes
- Ability, when changing jobs, to roll over your 401(k) or 403(b) balance to another plan or an IRA, or leave it with your previous employer (if the employer allows you to do so)

Consider all of these factors carefully, and, if necessary, seek outside professional help to answer any questions you may have. Most large companies will have staff on hand to help you with your concerns. Smaller companies frequently hire third-party administrators (TPAs) or outside financial services to assist their employees with these programs. Your employer will not make investment recommendations. You'll need to consult with the plan's financial advisor.

AMANDA'S STORY

When Amanda's husband died in middle age, she thought she was destitute. Amanda said she had only a $700-per-month pension on which to live.

As Amanda began to go through her husband's files, she discovered that her husband had saved over $500,000 in a 403(b) plan. Amanda was amazed. She said, "We spent all of my husband's paycheck." What Amanda didn't realize was that her husband had had the contribution deducted from his paycheck first. They did, indeed, spend all of his paycheck, but only what was left after his pretax savings. Smart man. This is why we encourage people to pay themselves first. The rewards are worth it.

And what a great relief it was for Amanda. She could at last relax, knowing she was well taken care of.

Keogh Plans

In the event that you are self-employed, be it full or part time, then you'll want to look into a Keogh plan—a tax-deferred savings plan much like an IRA. There are two different types of Keogh plans: a profit-sharing plan and a money purchase plan. There are regulations associated with a Keogh plan, and one of them is that a money purchase contribution is mandatory. This contribution must be of the same percentage each year regardless of your profits—even if you made none. With a profit-sharing plan, you can change your contribution amount each year. And there is no restriction preventing you from contributing to both plans in the same year.

Keogh contributions are tax deductible. The limit on what you can contribute will depend upon the version of Keogh you select. In some instances, you'll be able to contribute 25 percent of your net income. Keogh plans are a good choice for self-employed workers because the plan allows them to set aside the largest amount of money in a retirement program, sometimes up to $30,000 a year. Check with your advisor on the limits, as they may change.

Keogh earnings are also tax deferred, so until you make your withdrawal—which is assumed to be when you retire—you will not have to pay taxes on this money. When it does come time to make the withdrawal, your Keogh money will be taxed as ordinary income.

The Pros and Cons of Keogh Plans

Keogh plans offer a number of great advantages. They allow you to make pretax contributions, which reduces your annual income and your yearly taxes. Also, both your contributions and your earnings are tax deferred. Even though you invest in Keoghs, you can still invest in regular IRAs too.

One disadvantage of Keogh accounts is that they can be difficult to set up on your own because of their complexity. It's probably a good idea to work under the guidance of an expert so that you maximize your money and find a plan that is suited to your own needs.

You can make Keogh contributions for a given tax year. However, to claim a deduction for that given tax year, your Keogh account must be opened by December 31 or, if you are incorporated, by the end of your fiscal year.

WHEN TO PLAN FOR YOUR FUTURE

Planning for your future and your retirement needs requires some thinking in the here and now. Some people may be reluctant to start retirement planning. This reluctance may stem from insecurities about their finances and not knowing enough about the available options. If you find yourself feeling reluctant to start saving, talk with some of your friends. See if they have a financial advisor or have started their own retirement program. Or find a local seminar on retirement planning and attend it. Don't worry if it takes you time to understand all the ins and outs of retirement planning. Keep working at it.

Don't be intimidated by getting a plan in motion. Most experts will tell you that the bulk of your retirement future depends on the choices and decisions you make today. Do not delay making plans and building your retirement income.

There are a number of solid plans to choose from as well as a wealth of resources to help you find what's right for you. If you're concerned that you may not make the right choice, get help. Start saving today, stay focused on your goals, and try to participate in plans that allow you to generate additional wealth through tax-advantaged investing.

Visit our Web site at www.richandthinliving.com for a referral of investment advisors, financial advisors, or financial planners in your area.

8

Build Wealth with
a Healthy Credit Report

BEFORE YOU CAN BEGIN TO build wealth, you need to know what your credit report says about you. You need to get an assessment of your financial situation so you can set realistic, measurable financial goals and means of achieving them. It's just like with a diet, where you need to measure your weight to determine how much you need to lose.

It's essential to have a good credit report in order to buy real estate and other investments. More and more companies are looking at your credit report before approving you for insurance, rental of a home or apartment, employment, credit cards, and loans for automobiles and other uses. If there are blemishes on your report that are being reported, you may be denied employment, insurance, home, or automobile. That is why you want to be proactive and know what your credit report is saying about you before you ever complete an application for credit.

It's especially important to check your credit report from time to time to make sure that there are no inaccuracies being reported. If there are, it is up to you to fix them.

CHECKING YOUR CREDIT REPORT

A good rule to follow is to request a copy of your credit report from all three credit reporting agencies at least once a year. That way, you are prepared in advance for any purchase you may want to make. In any case, you should definitely check your report before applying for credit for a major purchase.

An added benefit of checking your credit report frequently is that you may be able to spot when someone has opened up bogus accounts in your name and is attempting to steal your identify. You should check the credit report frequently to find out what information merchants are getting when they make repeated credit inquiries on you. Merchants check up from time to time to see what is going on with your other accounts. Many times if they see anything that is questionable, such as late payments on these other accounts or a bankruptcy, they may feel threatened and increase your interest rate, close your account, or reduce your credit limit. So, you need to always know what is being said about you.

CREDIT REPORTING AGENCIES

There are three major credit reporting agencies in the United States: Experian, TransUnion, and Equifax. Each of these credit reporting agencies stores information in their computers on every individual who has a credit record. Creditors subscribe to the agencies, and report information to them monthly about individuals who have credit accounts with them.

Usually, such creditors are department stores, banks, and car dealerships. The county recorder's office records public records such as tax liens, judgments, and bankruptcies that may be reported by the credit reporting agencies. These subscribers do not report to all of the credit reporting agencies unless they are paying members. That is why an individual may have one item on only one credit report and not on the others. All positive or negative accounts will show up on the credit reports.

Do not confuse your local credit bureaus with the major credit reporting agencies. Your local credit bureaus are subsidiaries of the three national credit reporting agencies that store information. The local credit bureaus have access to Experian, TransUnion, and Equifax. In fact, many times the local credit bureaus will combine the information from all the major credit reporting agencies into one report. They often do so when a consumer is applying for a home loan. For that situation, more than one credit report is required.

LIMITS ON THE NEGATIVES

Credit entries, both good and bad, remain on the credit reporting agencies' files for only a limited amount of time. Once that time limit is up, the item must be removed. Here are the time limits for various items:

- Bankruptcies must be removed after 10 years from the date of filing.
- Judgments, paid tax liens, and most other unfavorable information such as slow pays, charge-offs, repossessions, delinquent accounts, and the like, must be removed seven years from the date of the last activity on your account.
- Good credit entries that have been closed or are no longer being used must also be removed after seven years from the date of closing or last use.
- A tax lien that is left unpaid can remain on your credit report indefinitely. If the lien is eventually paid, the record will stay on the credit report for seven years from the date the lien was paid.
- Inquiries that you make for new credit are listed on your credit report for up to two years from the date of the inquiry.

AUTHORIZATION

Many people are uncertain as to how a credit report about them came into being. They didn't authorize one, did they?

Guess what? You did it yourself and probably didn't realize it. Most types of applications you make for credit have a paragraph that states something like this:

> By signing below, I authorize XYZ company to check my credit history and exchange information about how I handle my account with proper persons and with credit bureaus if I am issued credit.

By signing this statement, you are authorizing a credit check and allowing the creditor to report your account to the credit reporting agencies.

NOT GIVING OUT INFORMATION

No one may get credit information from your credit file without direct permission from you. Be selective on whom you authorize to check your credit report. Here's a story from the coauthor that should give you pause.

HAL AND DEBORAH'S STORY

Many years ago, Hal and I were in the market for a new car, and we were on a hunt for the best deal. One afternoon I was walking through the kitchen and I heard Hal talking to someone on the phone. He was giving him his name, address, social security, number . . . basically, his life history.

Becoming alarmed, and being the "Credit Queen," I began jumping up and down, trying to get him to stop giving out that information. As any normal husband would do, he started waving his hand for me to be quiet. I couldn't believe he had given out his name, rank, and social security number!

When he hung up, he told me the guy he was talking to said he only needed the information for his files and he wasn't going to do anything with it.

Of course, I didn't trust the guy. We changed our minds about buying a car.

A few weeks later, I requested a copy of Hal's and my credit reports. Hal's credit report had four inquiries on the same date from the guy he spoke to regarding a car. Sure, he wasn't going to do anything with it! This was not a good thing, because, had Hal and I decided to continue with our purchase from another car agency, we might have been denied because of excessive inquiries on our report.

I made a phone call to the guy and introduced myself. I told him about the multiple inquiries on Hal's credit report and asked him who authorized him to run the credit report. He suddenly became quiet, began stuttering and stammering, and said no one gave him permission. My next response was, "I know my rights according to the Fair Credit Reporting Act, and would advise you to get all of these credit inquiries off the credit report." He was told that he had two weeks to do it and if the items weren't removed, I would contact an attorney. He said he didn't know how he was going to do it, as there were four banks involved. I told him I didn't care how he did it, but it must be done.

Somehow he managed to get all the inquiries off. The reason for his stammering and excuses was because he had violated the Fair Credit Reporting Act by running an unauthorized inquiry on Hal. The banks to which he submitted the application were also in violation of the act because of the unautho-rized information they had from the original company that this salesperson represented. This was a double whammy, requiring great effort to fix. But so what? Don't mess with the Credit Queen!

Most people don't know what their legal rights are. Don't allow yourself to be exploited and have others mess up your credit report and ruin your chances of gaining wealth through a great deal or investment.

GETTING YOUR OWN CREDIT REPORT

When applying for a car loan, home loan, or merchant credit, have your updated credit report on hand. Show that recent report to the potential creditor. Do not let them run a credit report on you unless they indicate your application will be approved. Doing so will eliminate the chance of having an inquiry on your report with an undesirable outcome. An inquiry can work against you if you do not qualify for the credit.

Now, wait a minute! Aren't you supposed to shop around for a good deal before making your purchase? What about trying to get the best interest rate? Shouldn't you be asking around at as many places as you can?

Be aware: five to six inquiries made within a six-month period may disqualify you from being approved for a purchase needing credit. Excess inquiries may lower your FICO score, which the lenders look at closely. We will examine FICO scores and how they work in more detail later (see "FICO Scores: They Can Make or Break You," below). When you are shopping for a major purchase such as a mortgage or automobile, the credit reporting agencies allow you a 14-day period to shop with other companies, and they will count those multiple inquiries as only one within that time frame. This benefit will reduce the number of inquiries that appear on your credit report, which may be reflected in your FICO score.

CREDIT DENIED

After you have applied for credit and your application has been turned down, the creditor must send you a letter within 60 days that states the reason you were denied the credit. The letter should include the name and address of the credit reporting agency that issued a credit report on your file. Whenever an application has been turned down, you are entitled to a free credit report from the credit reporting agency listed in the denial letter. You must request a copy of the credit report within 60 days of the denial letter. A copy of the denial letter should be included with your request. If the denial letter is not available, mention in your letter to the credit reporting agency the name of the company that refused you credit. (See the sample credit report request form.)

NOTE:

Don't try to get a free credit report from the other two credit reporting companies unless you know they also made an inquiry from the company you were trying to get credit from. If they did, go for it, and mention the creditor who denied you the credit.

GETTING A FREE CREDIT REPORT

The Fair and Accurate Credit Transactions Act (FACT Act) gives consumers the right to check their credit reports once a year for free. If you want your FICO or credit score, the credit reporting agency will charge a small fee. For more information, visit the Web site www.annualcreditreport.com or call 877-322-8228.

You are also entitled to a free credit report if you have been turned down for credit, employment, insurance, or a rental dwelling because of information in your credit report within the preceding 60 days.

HAVING YOUR OWN REPORT

Having an updated credit report from all the major credit reporting agencies that report in your community is a very good idea. One or more of the agencies—Experian, TransUnion, or Equifax—may be dominant in your area; each city and state is different. If you're unsure about which one is, you can call a bank or mortgage company to see from which company or companies they get their credit reports.

If you have not been turned down for credit, and you have already received your free annual credit report, the credit reporting agency will charge a fee for the report. Every state has its own fee. To find out what the fee is, call Experian, TransUnion, and Equifax directly or visit their Web sites. (See "Major Credit Bureaus" below for the contact information.)

When requesting a copy of your credit report, keep in mind that a husband and wife will not have combined reports. Each person has an individual report. This situation applies even if most (or all) of the accounts are joint accounts. After each of you receives your annual free credit report, you must pay fees for each report you receive thereafter—for example, you might have to pay $8 for the husband and $8 for the wife.

ORDERING YOUR CREDIT REPORT

When requesting a copy of your credit report, you will need to include the following information.

- Full name, including middle initial and generation, such as Jr., Sr., II, or III.
- Address with zip code.
- Previous address with zip code, if you have moved within the last five years.
- Social security number.
- Date of birth.
- Spouse's name.
- For verification purposes, a photocopy of a billing statement, driver's license, or other document that links your name with the requested report and the address to which it is to be mailed. Some bureaus require two forms of identification.

You can order your credit report directly from the credit reporting agency's Web site, by writing a letter to the agency, or by calling the agency's toll-free number.

On the reverse side of your credit report, there will be instructions telling you how to read each account and informing you how you are being rated. Make sure the items are being accurately reported. Many times there is inaccurate information on your credit report that must be corrected before you can apply for credit.

Credit bureaus are regulated by the Federal Trade Commission under the provisions of the federal Fair Credit Reporting Act, the Consumer Credit Reporting Reform Act of 1996, and the Fair and Accurate Credit Transactions Act. To receive a copy of each of the laws, write to the Federal Trade Commission, 600 Pennsylvania Ave., N.W., Washington, DC 20580.

MAJOR CREDIT BUREAUS

Here are the addresses of the national headquarters of Experian, TransUnion, and Equifax. You may request copies of your credit report from these agencies, or refer to your phone directory for the phone numbers and addresses of the credit reporting agencies in your area.

Equifax:
P.O. Box 740241, Atlanta, GA 30374
(800) 685-1111
www.equifax.com

Experian:
P.O. Box 2104, Allen, TX 75013

(888) 397-3742
www.experian.com

TransUnion:
P.O. Box 1000, Chester, PA 19022
(800) 888-4213
www.transunion.com

To find your local credit bureau, look in your telephone directory. If you are unable to locate one near you, write to the headquarters to receive your credit report.

FREE ANNUAL CREDIT REPORT

To receive your free annual credit reports under the Fair and Accurate Credit Transactions Act, visit www.annual creditreport.com or call 877-322-8228.

Sample Credit Report Request Form

Experian
PO Box 2104
Allen, TX 75013

Please send me a free annual credit report.

Name

Address

City, State, Zip

Previous address (last five years)

Social Security Number

Year of Birth

Thank you,

Sign name

(Use this format if you have not been turned down for credit recently.)

Enclose a copy of your driver's license or a bill (such as a utility bill) that has your name and address.

TransUnion
PO Box 1000
Chester, PA 19022

Please send me a copy of my current credit report. I am enclosing the necessary fee of $8.00 for my report.

Name

Address

City, State, Zip

Previous address (last five years)

Social Security Number

Year of Birth

Thank you,

(Use this format if you have not been turned down for credit recently.)

Enclose a copy of your driver's license or a bill (such as a utility bill) that has your name and address.

Sample Credit Report Request Form

Equifax
P.O. Box 740241
Atlanta, GA 30374-0241

Please send me a copy of my current credit report. I have been recently turned down for credit by: _____.

Name

Address

City, State, Zip

Previous Address (last five years)

Social Security Number

Year of Birth

Thank you,

Sign name

(Use this format if you have been turned down for credit within the last 60 days.)

STEPS FOR EVALUATING CREDIT RECORDS
AND DISPUTING REPORTED ITEMS

Don't be intimidated by the prospect of evaluating your credit report and disputing any items mentioned in it. The first thing to do is to obtain a copy of your report from the three major reporting agencies: Experian, TransUnion, and Equifax. Complete your request forms and mail them to all three agencies. Remember, you can also make these requests online, through their Web sites.

Once you have a credit report in hand, you're ready to evaluate it ... and amend it, if necessary. Here's how to go about doing that.

Step 1

Determine the status of your credit file by analyzing all the items that are being reported. Look to see if the accounts are being reported 100 percent accurately. For example, check account numbers, status, amount, dates, and all pertinent data.

You need to dispute all inaccurate, incomplete, and erroneous information that is showing on the report. There will be a key to use on the credit report to help you in determining the negative items. When disputing any information, use the sample response form (Form #2) for any excuse you may have or reasons you think the information is inaccurate.

Step 2

Write a letter or use the forms provided by Experian, TransUnion, or Equifax for disputing inaccurate entries.

You can also dispute any information online, via the individual credit reporting agencies' Web sites. Do not mention more than four to six inaccurate entries on any one dispute letter or form. If you are mailing your dispute letter, mail one letter, via regular mail, disputing the claims every 30 days to the agency making the report. *Notice the mailing dates* in our sample letters. These dates are important; they give the time frame in which you need to send and resend letters disputing items reported to the agency. Be sure to keep copies of all the letters you send. Also, the dates will help you track the length of time the credit reporting agency takes to update its records.

The credit reporting agencies will complete their investigation with the creditors within 30 days from receipt of your dispute letter. If the creditors fail to respond to the credit bureau within that time period, by federal law the item must be removed from the credit file. If the item is unverifiable or incorrect, the item being disputed on the credit report must be corrected or removed from the credit report.

You should receive a copy of your updated credit report within 45 to 60 days of your letter through the mail. It should indicate any changes on the report.

Step 3

When you receive a copy of your updated credit report, note what changes have been made. You should see some changes, but occasionally not all the items are removed the first time. Don't be discouraged. Repeat Step 2 a second time. Mention only the remaining erroneous items in the letter, and mail it (or dispute via the credit reporting agency's Web site) 120 days or later from the date you received the last updated report. You can repeat this procedure as often as you want, but remember to time the mailings or Web site disputes at least 120 days from receipt of each report.

If you do not wish to continue the letter writing, you can include a 100-word statement on each entry that explains your side of the story. See the sample "100-Word Statement" below.

Things to Remember

1. Request credit reports from the appropriate agencies.
2. Enclose a fee for the report if you are requesting it for a reason other than denial of credit, if you have already received your annual credit report, or if you are requesting your FICO score.
3. A husband and wife must request separate credit reports.
4. Analyze all negative, inaccurate, and incomplete information.
5. If the credit reporting agency has dispute forms, use these forms. If not, write a letter using one of the samples that appear in this book.
6. If you are using the Internet, print copies with the date the dispute was sent.
7. Make sure all letters have the date written on them.
8. Review all updated reports.
9. Repeat the process, if necessary.
10. Be patient and persistent.

Sample Responses

1. I do not recall having this account. This is not mine.
2. I do not believe I was ever 30 (60, 90, or however many) days late on this account.
3. I paid this account in full as agreed. It was not a charge-off.
4. This is not my bankruptcy. [insert date and amount]
5. I do not owe this judgment for $ amount _____.
6. I do not owe this tax lien for $ amount _____.
7. This account was the responsibility of my SEPARATED or DIVORCED spouse.

It is not recommended that you make up a fictitious story! What you are trying to do is cause an investigation of the inaccurate information being reported on the credit report and see that it will be removed or corrected. The sample responses can be used, or you can write one that will be appropriate for your situation. The more of your personality that is projected, the better the letter.

Sample Dispute Letters

Form #2

June 19, 20____

Dear Credit Bureau,

After receiving a copy of my credit report I have found incorrect information being reported.

My account at XYZ company, account #111111, was paid in full as agreed and was not a charge-off. Please remove this.

I never paid Kelly Co. 60 days late. Account #12344. Please correct this.

This Tax Lien Docket #555555 was paid in full. I do not owe this.

My name is John Doe, and I reside at 2233 Park Ave., Anytown, CA 22222. My social security number is 111-22-3333. My previous address was 6143 Summer Ln., Anytown, CA 22222. My birth date is 11-17-1980.

Sincerely,

John Doe

[Remember to personalize your letters!]

Sample Dispute Letter Form #2

[Note: This date is 30 days later than the previous one.]

July 19, 20____

Dear Credit Bureau,

After receiving my credit report and checking my records, I have found information that is not correct. My name is John Doe, and I reside at 2233 Park Ave., Anytown, CA 22222. My social security number is 111-22-3333. My previous address was 6143 Summer Ln., Anytown, CA 22222. My birth date is 11/17/1980.

I do not have an account with Brewer's Collection, account #12456.

My account at Nelson's Dept. Store, #4441, was paid in full as agreed and should have a positive rating.

This bankruptcy, docket #45667, for $100,000.00, 10-12-00 is wrong and should not be on my report. This is not mine.

Sincerely,

John Doe

[Remember to personalize your letters!]

Sample 100-Word Statement

October 13, 20____

To Whom It May Concern,

Please add this statement to my credit profile. Make this a part of my credit report.

In May 2005, I was laid off from my job due to an injury. I fell behind on my payments. It took me four months to get back on the job, but my debts had become seriously delinquent. I made arrangements with my creditors to repay these debts. I have since paid them all off and am in good standing. My job is secure, and I am now trying to rebuild my credit.

My name is John Smith. I reside at 2398 Main St., Anytown, MN 33333. My social security number is 333-88-9999. My previous address was 1245 Maple, Anytown, MN 33444. My birth date is 5/8/1975.

Sincerely,

Sign name

FICO SCORES: THEY CAN MAKE OR BREAK YOU

A FICO score is commonly used throughout the lending industry to quickly identify whether a potential applicant is creditworthy. So when someone applies for a credit card, mortgage, or bank loan, the creditor will check both the credit report and the FICO score. The initials are derived from the scoring system developed by Fair, Isaac & Co.

There are other credit bureau scores besides the FICO score, and some lenders may incorporate a FICO score into their own system. In an Equifax report, the FICO score can also be referred to as a BEACON score. Experian uses the Experian/Fair Isaac Risk Model, and TransUnion has the EMPIRICA score. FICO scores are the most common term used throughout the lending industry.

The FICO score is calculated using several different variables that can be grouped into five categories. Each category makes up a percentage of the score.

35% – Payment history
30% – Amounts owed
15% – Length of credit history

10% – Types of credit used
10% – New credit

This information is averaged into a three-digit number. These scores can range from 300 to 850. Most lenders prefer to see a score of 700 or above for credit approval. Scores above 620 will still get consumers good rates.

The points allocated to your FICO score are *top secret!* No one knows exactly how many points each factor is worth. You can visit www.MYFICO.com to view your score and have an analysis done.

There are ways you can improve your FICO scores. Here are some suggestions.

- Always pay your bills on time. This will help create a good payment pattern. Payment history makes up the largest portion of the score.
- Keep your balances on your credit cards low. It is best if the credit balance is 30 percent or less of your credit limit. To pay down your credit card debt, save where you can on your expenses. Refer to the Money Calorie Counter in Chapter 2 for ideas. Use the money you are saving to pay down credit card debt.
- Do not apply for more credit than you need.
- Excessive inquiries on a credit report can lower your score. An inquiry basically shows that a creditor or potential creditor ran your credit report.
- Too many open accounts on your credit report may cause you to be viewed as a credit risk by potential lenders.

- If you are going to close accounts, you should keep old accounts open and close the newer accounts. The best solution is to keep all accounts open, but don't use them.
- Finance companies can also lower a FICO score. The reason is that a finance company is usually used by higher credit risk individuals. When a borrower uses a finance company, he or she is often assumed to have been turned down for a lower interest rate loan.

IT'S WORTH IT TO CLEAN IT UP!

A good credit report is a must in getting what you want on your road to wealth. It's one of the most essential tools in this *Rich and Thin* book. It can make or break you. So… *have a good credit report* so you can achieve the dreams and goals you want in your life.

9

Gain Wealth in Real Estate

THE AMERICAN DREAM IS TO own a home. The way to gain wealth is to own a home plus invest in other properties that will go up in value.

Owning a home is like a "forced savings." Each time you make a house payment, the principal on your loan goes down. There has been a tremendous appreciation in real estate over the past several years. Property values have multiplied. For example, a home that sold several years ago for $250,000 is now worth $450,000. With a balance of $200,000, that gives you $250,000 of equity in your home. If you sold your home, you would net $250,000 less your costs. Not bad!

Real estate doesn't have the highs and lows that stocks do. It usually is a steady growth of equity. Even if there is a down market and property values are decreasing, if you hang onto your property, it will eventually go back up.

There are loan programs that offer you no money down or as little as 5 to 10 percent down even for investment properties. It is important to know what programs are out there for you in qualifying.

When looking for real estate as an investment, look for areas that have potential growth. Remember the rule: location, location, location! Here's a story from the coauthor's experience.

MELINDA'S STORY

A few months before Mike and I got married, Mike decided to look into buying a home. He had a new job and was relocating to a new area. Mike found a new subdivision that he liked and put money down on a house to be built. I was still in college at the time, and the thought of owning a home sounded frightening. Of course, I gave him my input: don't do it; let's back out of the deal! I thought we should rent an apartment instead.

After many discussions, Mike convinced me that buying a house was a better option for us. We bought the home for $130,000 in Scottsdale, Arizona. Three years later, we sold the home for $190,000. We used some of our proceeds for the down payment on a bigger house and put money aside for other real estate investments. Now we own our home and have also purchased several investment properties from the equity we have gained over the years. To this day, Mike likes to tease

LOOK FOR GREAT DEALS

Look for great deals. Contact a real estate company that specializes in foreclosures. Read your newspaper classified ads for properties offered "For Sale By Owner." Many times an owner may need to sell quickly and not hire a real estate company to save on costs. Another way to find great deals is to go to the county recorder's office to see defaults filed (banks filing foreclosures) and recorded. You can then contact the owner directly to see if you can make the purchase. Another person's hardship may be your reward in the real estate hunt.

We have also found that brand-new homes will appreciate quickly. If you are in the market for a brand-new home, try and get in on the early phase releases. Those usually have your best prices. Many new home developments will also sell to investors as well as potential homeowners.

One way to secure a house for investment is to look for a new home. There are many people who have had credit challenges and can't qualify yet for a home loan but will within 12 to 24 months. They may have the money for a down payment but not be able to qualify for a good loan. You can work a "purchase option" with them, where you buy the house, then rent the home back to them. They can pay you an agreed-upon amount of option money in advance, plus the rent and secure a sales price at which they will buy the home within a certain time frame. By doing this, you have an agreed sales price, advance money that is nonrefundable, and a person living in the property paying you rent that is applied to the payment. A certain amount of the rent payment will be applied to the purchase. If the time comes and they cannot fulfill the purchase option, they forfeit the option money and you are free to do what you want with the property.

Looking for a home or investment? Need to prequalify for a mortgage? Visit our Web site to get in contact with a real estate professional in your area: www.richandthin living.com.

Many people become millionaires through real estate. They know how to find a good deal and make their money grow. This is also a great way to be able to liquidate your money if needed for retirement or to reinvest.

APPLYING FOR A LOAN

When you are applying for credit, the credit grantor will be looking for several things before granting you a line of credit. Credit may be obtained with a credit card, a mortgage for a house, a car, or a loan. Creditors look for an ability to repay the debt and a willingness to do so. Creditors are looking for the "three C's" of credit: capacity, character, and collateral. Let's examine each one of these factors.

Capacity

The creditor wants to make sure you can repay the debt. To qualify you on the initial application, creditors will ask questions regarding your employment, as well as the length of time you have been employed. Creditors want to know what your total income is, including any bonuses. They also want to know how much your expenses are, how many dependents you have, and if you are paying any child support or alimony.

How do creditors calculate your debt capacity? They use a standard formula called a debt to income ratio. They start by calculating your total monthly debt or expenses. This includes such items as your car payments, homeowner's insurance, property taxes, credit card payments, alimony, child support, proposed new mortgage payment, and homeowner's association (HOA) fees if applicable. Your current rent or mortgage payment is not included. This figure will equal the amount of your monthly debt. When figuring this number, creditors include the monthly payment of the item that you want to finance. Next, they'll divide this number by your total monthly gross (before taxes) income.

The following is an example of how the debt to income ratio is calculated:

Total Gross Monthly Income: $4,000
Total Monthly Debt, Including Proposed Loan
    Payment: $1,600
Debt to Income Ratio: $1,600/$4,000 = 40%

The total monthly payments, $1,600, divided by the total monthly gross income, $4,000, equals your debt to income ratio, 40 percent. If the ratio is over 50 percent, most likely the banks will not approve the loan. Before you apply for credit, speak with the lending institution about what its policies are concerning debt to income ratio.

Debt to Income Calculation

Gross Monthly Income		Monthly Fixed Expenses	
Salary	$_____	Rent or mortgage	$_____
Spouse salary	_____	Automobile	_____
Commissions	_____	Automobile	_____
Bonuses	_____	Bank installments	_____
Alimony	_____	Charge/Revolving	_____
Child Support	_____	Child support	_____
Other	_____	Alimony	_____
Other	_____		
Total income	$_____	Other	_____
(Before taxes)		Proposed loan payment	_____
		Total payments	$_____

The total monthly payments _____ divided by the total monthly gross income _____ equals your debt ratio _____.

Character

When attempting to determine your qualification for a loan, creditors will look at your credit history and your paying habits. Usually they can get this information through one of the three credit reporting agencies: Experian, TransUnion, and Equifax. Creditors are also looking for stability. They will look at the length of time you have lived at your current address, and whether you own or rent your home.

Basically, the creditors want to know if they are protected should you stop payment on the loan or debt. Showing the assets you have, other than job income, can put creditors' minds at ease. Such assets could be savings accounts, investments, or property owned.

OTHER FACTORS IN QUALIFYING FOR A LOAN

Creditors use different combinations of these factors to reach their decision. They also use different kinds of rating systems. Here are the major factors creditors look for:

1. Sufficient monthly income
2. Number of years on the job
3. Good payment record on past debts
4. Checking and/or savings account
5. Monthly debt obligations

Talk to the lender before applying for a loan. Find out what factors the lender uses to make its evaluation; each lender has different ones.

To find out how to be prequalified for a mortgage, visit our Web site: www.richandthinliving.com.

FICO SCORES AND QUALIFYING
FOR A REAL ESTATE LOAN

As mentioned in the previous chapter, prior to submitting an application for a mortgage, find out your FICO score. You can request a copy directly from all of the credit reporting agencies: TransUnion, Equifax, and Experian. By requesting a copy of your credit reports, along with your FICO scores, you will avoid having the potential creditor make an unwanted inquiry. Note: there will be an additional fee when you request your FICO score. Refer to "FICO Scores: They Can Make or Break You" in Chapter 8 for more information.

CREDIT RESCORING

If your FICO score is low, you may want to check into the services of a credit rescorer. A credit rescore service is a relatively new type of service being offered by local credit reporting agencies nationwide. You'll need to check local listings to see if such a service is offered in your area. The three large credit bureaus, Equifax, Experian, and TransUnion, are not affiliated with this service.

How does credit rescoring work? A rescorer goes through your files, carefully reviewing any negative entries you may have. Sometimes, these "derogatories" are simply inaccuracies or errors. The rescorer goes through and obtains written corrections of these entries, and then sends them to the three credit reporting agencies.

Rescorers will also look at your current debt. They'll evaluate your situation and advise you on how you can restructure certain information—the kind that may have caused a creditor to reject your loan application. For example, you may have high outstanding balances on your credit cards. You don't want high credit card balances when having your FICO scores pulled. So the rescorer will advise you on how to redistribute or pay off these balances so that your application will be approved. Such advice can result in a raised FICO score. Ask your lender to refer you to a reliable rescoring expert.

When you are attempting to qualify for a refinance or mortgage, most mortgage companies require a *mortgage factual*. This is a credit report in which the husband's and wife's credit, plus two or three of the credit bureaus' information, are merged together into one report. It's crucial that you know exactly what each bureau says about you. If your TransUnion credit report does not look good, but your Experian and Equifax reports look better, ask the mortgage company to run only those reports.

The company that is running a mortgage factual will also verify your social security number, employment, and previous inquiries. They will do a thorough investigation on you.

To avoid getting inquiries on your credit report when applying for a car or home, or any type of merchant credit, have an updated credit report with your FICO score on hand to show the creditor or bank. They can evaluate the report immediately without running another report, and thus avoid another inquiry being added to your credit file. If they indicate that the application will be approved, then go ahead and authorize them to run a credit report.

LENDERS' REQUIREMENTS

When filling out the credit application, be sure to list the items that you know are on your credit report. Make sure that the income you state on your application can be verified with your employer.

The lender will require two years of past federal tax returns with W-2 forms and a copy of your last two pay stubs. This information will be compared with your listed income.

Lenders usually require self-employed individuals to provide a complete personal and business federal tax return for the past two years, plus a current year-to-date profit and loss statement.

If you own rental property, a copy of all your rental agreements with a list of the real estate owned will be required. You must provide this information whether you are refinancing your own residence or a rental property.

A copy of your award letter is required if you receive pension or social security income. You must also supply the lender with a copy of the most recent check received or bank statements showing direct deposits.

Divorced applicants must provide a complete copy of the final divorce decree and a marital settlement, if applicable.

If you have filed a past bankruptcy, a copy of the discharge papers must be given to the lender.

Copies of your last three bank statements for each bank account listed on your application may be requested for verification.

Stock, IRA, 401(k), or any other investment statements you have listed on the application may be requested for review.

LOAN SUBMISSION

Once your mortgage application is submitted, within three days of its receipt, you will receive additional disclosure forms. The disclosure forms will require your signature to indicate that you have verified the information listed on the application. The two disclosure forms are the Good Faith Estimate (GFE) of settlement costs and the Truth in Lending disclosure.

Good Faith Estimate of Settlement Costs

This is an estimate of most of the charges you will be required to pay at the closing of your loan. If you are purchasing a home and require a new loan, these costs will be included as your closing costs and down payment. These costs must be paid at the close of escrow in the form of a cashier's check.

If you are refinancing your home, the estimated closing costs will be added back into your loan. This amount will increase the loan you are refinancing. Other than the credit report fee and the appraisal fee, no out-of-pocket expenses are required. It is all included in your loan. Occasionally, the credit report fee and appraisal fee may also be included in your loan.

The costs shown on the Good Faith Estimate are subject to change. For instance, a purchase or refinance that closes at the end of the month will have cheaper closing costs than one that closes at other times. Why is that so? The prepaid interest on the loan is less because it is computed on a daily basis, so you are charged only for the amount of days remaining in the month. If you were to close your loan on the twenty-seventh day of the month, you would only be charged three to four days worth of interest. On the other hand, if you were to close the loan on the first day of the month, you would be charged for the remaining 29 to 30 days.

Your mortgage payment is always paid in arrears. For example, a payment made on March 1 covers the month of February. When you close your loan, the prepaid interest covers the days remaining for that month. You would not make a payment the following month. For example, if you closed your loan on April 15, you would pay 15 days of prepaid interest. Your first payment would be June 1, which covers the month of May.

Truth in Lending Disclosure

Federal law requires that all consumers receive a Truth in Lending (TIL) disclosure statement before any consumer credit transaction is completed. The TIL will show you what the annual percentage rate (APR) is and how much the payments will be for the duration of the loan. It also tabulates all the costs involved in the loan, thus usually making the APR appear higher than the actual interest rate you will be paying. The interest rate in your final loan papers, called the Note, will have the actual interest rate, which should be lower. Familiarize yourself thoroughly with what is contained in the statement, as it will affect what goes on during the life of the loan and how much you will ultimately pay. Here are some things you will encounter in Truth in Lending disclosures and should review prior to signing any documents.

Prepaid finance charges. Loan charges paid by the borrower. Prepaid finance charges could include loan origination fees, discount and commitment fees, prepaid mortgage insurance premium (PMI) for conventional loans (PMI is an insurance required by the lender for loans with less than 20 percent down or less than 20 percent equity on a refinance), FHA mortgage insurance premium (MIP) for FHA loans, VA funding fees, and prepaid interest.

Annual percentage rate (APR). Not the same thing as the *note interest rate*, if there are any prepaid finance charges. The APR reflects those charges and gives you a way to measure and compare the effective annual cost of the loan.

Finance charges. The total cost of credit as a dollar amount. It is the total prepaid finance charges plus total interest and mortgage insurance premiums paid over the life of the loan according to the payment schedule. For adjustable rate loans, the finance charge will be subject to change if the interest rate varies.

Amount financed. Not the same thing as the *loan amount*. It is the amount requested by you (including any MIP to be financed) less prepaid finance charges paid at closing.

Total of payment. The amount you will have paid after you have made all of your scheduled payments.

Prepayment penalty. A fee that is charged if you pay off your loan early. If there is a prepayment penalty, it will be stated in your loan documents.

Remember! Review these items carefully, to make sure that you are getting the terms that you want and negotiated for.

TYPES OF LOANS
AVAILABLE

There are numerous types of loans available for both new purchases and refinances.

Conventional Loan

Conventional loans are nongovernmental loans that are primarily made by banks, savings and loans, and other financial institutions. There are two varieties of conventional loans, conforming and nonconforming.

A *conforming loan* is any conventional loan under $417,000 (as of 2007). The Federal National Mortgage Association (FNMA), commonly known as "Fannie Mae," and the Federal Home Loan Mortgage Corporation (FHLMC), commonly known as "Freddie Mac"—two organizations that create affordable housing through partnerships—can purchase a conforming loan on a wholesale basis. A *nonconforming loan*, also known as a *jumbo loan*, is used for any amount over $417,000 for one unit (as of 2007). The Federal Housing Administration (FHA) and the Department of Veterans Affairs (VA) have different loan limits subject to the city locations. These loans are usually less than conforming loans. Periodically, Fannie Mae and Freddie Mac will increase the maximum loan amounts. Be sure to find out the current amounts from your lender.

Fixed Loan

A fixed loan is one where the interest rate remains the same throughout the duration of the loan. Stated simply, the interest rate will not change. A fixed interest rate loan is a good choice if the interest rates are low.

Stated Income Loan
(also known as an *easy loan* or *no doc loan*)

A stated income loan requires little documentation to prove a borrower's assets or income. This type of loan is commonly used for a borrower who is self-employed or who works in service industries. A borrower's credit score usually has to be a little higher for a stated income loan than for a regular loan. A lender will generally charge a slightly higher interest rate and fee for this type of loan, and in some cases, it may limit the loan to 70 to 75 percent of the value of the home.

Adjustable Rate Mortgage (ARM)

An ARM begins at a lower rate of interest, which will adjust every six months or once a year. The final note you sign will give you the details of when the adjustments will occur. The rate of adjustment is based on the index plus the margin. The *index* is a rate that is recognized by financial markets such as Treasury bills, LIBOR rate, Federal Reserve Cost of Funds Index, certificates of deposit, and the prime rate. The margin is established by the lender or the investor. It can be from 0 basis points to 2 or 3 points or even higher.

To determine the interest rate, add the index to the margin set by the investor. The total will be the interest rate charged. For example, if the index is 5 and the margin is 2½, the interest rate would be 7½ percent.

The advantage of this type of loan is that the payment is lower in the beginning of the loan term.

Adjustable Rate Mortgage with a Fixed Rate
for a Certain Time Period

An ARM may be set at a fixed interest rate for 3, 5, 7, or 10 years, then adjust. The amount of years the loan is fixed is determined in your contract or note with the lender. When the term of the fixed rate has been completed, the payment becomes adjustable.

The average person moves or refinances his or her home every five years. This program is a good option for savings if you do not plan on living in the property long term or keeping the loan.

Graduated Mortgage Payment (GMP)

A GMP has a fixed pay schedule, with the payment being fixed at one-year intervals for a total of five years. The payment adjusts one time per year for five years. When the loan is made, there is a schedule of payments for each year so you will know what to expect.

The advantage to this type of loan is that you can qualify for a higher value home with less income.

This type of loan carries a possible negative amortization and will readjust after the fifth year. A negative amortization means your balance can be higher than what you started out with.

Community Home Buyers Loan

This type of loan, sponsored by the Community Home Buyers program of Fannie Mae, is conventional financing. The borrower has to complete a questionnaire after reading a booklet. This loan has a fixed rate and requires a low down payment. It is more competitive than FHA financing. Some flexibility is allowed for credit problems and lower incomes, similar to FHA loans.

FHA Loan

There are several different types of government-backed loans available through the Federal Housing Administration (FHA). FHA insures the loan, making it a lower risk for the lender.

The advantage of an FHA insured loan is the low down payment required, plus most lenders are flexible with individuals who have had credit problems.

The disadvantage is that FHA insured loans do not have high loan amounts compared to conventional loans.

VA Loan

To qualify for a VA-backed loan, you must have served in the military. In most cases a down payment is not required with a VA loan.

Negative Amortization
Adjustable Rate

This type of loan rate is the index plus the margin [refer to "Adjustable Rate Mortgage (ARM)"], but it will start with an initial lower rate. The payment can only increase, in most cases, 7.5 percent per year. The adjustment of the rate can occur every month, every 6 months, or every 12 months.

The advantage of this type of loan is that you can qualify for more house with less income. This frees up more money for savings or investments. This type of loan is not good in a down market or in a situation where the property values are dropping.

The disadvantage to this type of loan is a negative amortization. The negative amount is added to the balance. To avoid a negative amortization, add more money each month to the payment.

Reverse Mortgage

This type of loan is good for individuals over the age of 62 who do not owe anything on their home or have a large amount of equity in their property. The older you are, the more money you receive. This loan will allow you to pull out a lump sum, create a line of credit, or pay you a certain amount of money each month. There are no payments on this loan. When you die, move out of the property, or sell the house, the bank will get paid back what is owed on the balance and you or your heirs will receive the remaining equity. Go to www.legacymoney.com for more details.

Equity Line of Credit

An equity line of credit will allow you to take out money for any purpose. When setting up this type of loan, you can take out zero dollars or whatever you need to borrow. There will be a limit on what you can take out, but you pay back only what is borrowed. The rates are usually adjustable and long term.

Second Trust Deed

When applying for a second trust deed, the lender will qualify you as if you were applying for a new loan. An appraisal is done to find out how much equity is in the property, which will determine the amount you can borrow. The interest rate is usually higher on a second trust deed. Many lenders will allow you 10 to 30 years to pay back the loan.

DOCUMENTATION REQUIRED FOR
PURCHASE OF A HOME OR INVESTMENT

The purchase of a house is probably one of the largest investments a person will ever make. Many people who decide to purchase a home have no idea what factors a lender or mortgage company will consider when attempting to approve the loan.

The **down payment** required will be based upon the type of loan that is being requested. No matter what type of loan you seek, the lender will always be looking at certain criteria. You will have to fill out many forms, including the initial credit application, verification of employment, and verification of deposit.

The **credit application** you will complete will require information about you and your spouse or coborrower. It has a section similar to a financial statement that must be filled out completely. Be sure to list all of your assets in this section. Mention all the property owned, such as cars, furniture, jewelry, and silver. Include anything that will add to your net worth. Usually when listing your liabilities (or debts you owe), the lender will not consider any debts that will be paid off within the next 10 months.

Know what items are on each of your credit reports. If you have had problems in the past with credit, it is best to tell the lender about that right away. Lack of communication will cause denials on loan applications. Occasionally a letter of explanation may be all that is required regarding a negative item on your report. In most cases, it is easier to get approved for a home loan than for a credit card. The reason? Because the house is the security for the mortgage.

Verification of employment is a form that the lender will send to your employer verifying where you work. It is a questionnaire your employer or other such authorized person fills out. It will ask the length of employment and the base amount of pay per hour or per month. The amount of overtime pay, bonuses, and commissions will also be asked. The lender is looking for at least two years of employment at the same job. However, if a person has been employed, let's say, for two months at a new job, but was employed by another company prior to this one doing the same type of work for at least two years, it still counts as a suitable length of employment. The lender will also send a verification of employment to any other job you have had within the past two years. Any time a person changes employment to better himself or herself financially, the lender will be satisfied. When an individual has had a break in employment for several months or quits several jobs and shows no stability, then the lender will question the application. They may ask for a letter of explanation or possibly reject the loan. Every lender is different.

The **Verification of Deposit** form is mailed to the bank(s) listed on the application. The bank(s) must fill out the form and will indicate the current balance and average daily balance of your accounts. The form is then returned to the mortgage company, where it becomes an important part of the loan package.

When you are applying for a loan to purchase a house, the loan company does not allow you to borrow any money for your down payment or closing costs. If you are short on the down payment, occasionally the lender will allow a relative to give you the money, provided that person writes a letter or statement that indicates that it is a gift and does not need to be repaid. This is called a *gift letter*.

PROPERTY APPRAISAL

Another important part of the loan package is the property appraisal. At the beginning of the loan process, the lender will usually ask for a check to cover the costs of your credit report and appraisal. Both fees are nonrefundable. The lender will assign an appraiser to go out and look at the property. The property will be compared with other homes in the area. A market study will then be done to determine the value of the property.

When a home is purchased, an ideal situation would be for the property to be appraised at the price at which you bought it. If the property has an appraised value lower than the purchase price, the bank will loan only a percentage of the appraised value. In that case, you, the purchaser, may choose to pay over the appraised value or renegotiate with the seller. If the seller does not wish to renegotiate, you are not obligated to complete the sale. However, if the property is appraised for more than the purchase price, the original deal remains the same and the lender will base the down payment on the selling price. Very seldom is a property appraised for more than the sales price, because the appraiser knows the sales price before the appraisal is conducted.

When an appraisal is done for a purchase or refinance, the appraiser will do an analysis and a review of the properties that have recently sold in the area. The value will be determined by a comparison of similar properties with the same square footage, lot size, and comparable amenities.

A slow economy may cause many property values to drop. For a refinance, there must be enough equity (meaning the difference between the loan owed and the appraised value) for the lender to approve the loan. The loan to value (LTV) ratio on a refinance needs to be between 65 and 100 percent, depending on other criteria such as your credit rating and income. Each lender has specific stipulations.

Once the credit report, verification of employment, verification of deposits, and appraisal are complete, the loan package is ready to be submitted to the underwriter (the lender) for final approval.

FOUR-TO-ONE RULE

A good rule to use in qualifying for your house payment is the four-to-one rule, meaning your monthly payment does not exceed four times your monthly gross income. For example, if your house payment is $1,000 per month, then your gross monthly income should be at least $4,000 Every lender has different ratios. Be sure and discuss it with the lender at the time of application.

There are some lenders who will allow you a 50 percent ratio when qualifying, meaning that your monthly payment can equal 50 percent of your monthly gross.

RAPID MORTGAGE REDUCTION

There are several ways to become wealthy in real estate. One way to build your wealth more quickly is to pay off your mortgage early by making one extra monthly payment per year. Let's say your payment is $1,900 per month. You can either make one extra payment per year or divide the payment per month. For example, if your payment is $1,900 per month and you add $158.33 more to each monthly payment, your total monthly payment will be $2,058.33. By paying that amount monthly, your 30-year loan will be paid off in 23 years. Another way to set this up would be to pay biweekly. Split your payment in half and make a payment every other week. This will create one extra payment per year.

Make sure when adding more money to your payments that you make a note that the amount needs to be credited to principal.

Here's how your mortgage would be paid down more quickly—and you would save in the long run—if you made extra payments per year. Review the Mortgage Reduction example to see the years reduced and your savings.

Mortgage Reduction Example

Based on 6 percent interest rate, $100,000 loan amount, 30 years (amounts in US$) with a loan start date of March 2002.

Year	Loan Balance		Yearly Interest Paid		Yearly Principal Paid		Total Interest	
	Biweekly	Standard	Biweekly	Standard	Biweekly	Standard	Biweekly	Standard
2002	98,444.51	98,981.79	5,039.57	4,977.30	1,555.49	1,018.21	5,039.57	4,977.30
2003	96,501.56	97,690.98	5,851.21	5,903.79	1,942.95	1,290.81	10,890.77	10,881.09
2004	94,438.60	96,320.56	5,731.20	5,824.18	2,062.95	1,370.43	16,621.97	16,705.27
2005	92,248.23	94,865.60	5,603.79	5,739.65	2,190.37	1,454.95	22,225.76	22,444.93
2006	89,922.58	93,320.91	5,468.50	5,649.92	2,325.65	1,544.69	27,694.26	28,094.84
2007	87,453.29	91,680.95	5,324.86	5,554.64	2,469.29	1,639.96	33,019.13	33,649.49
2008	84,831.48	89,939.84	5,172.35	5,453.49	2,621.80	1,741.11	38,191.48	39,102.98
2009	82,047.75	88,091.34	5,010.42	5,346.11	2,783.73	1,848.50	43,201.90	44,449.09
2010	79,092.08	86,128.83	4,838.49	5,232.09	2,955.67	1,962.51	48,040.39	49,681.18
2011	75,953.86	84,045.27	4,655.94	5,111.05	3,138.22	2,083.56	52,696.33	54,792.23
2012	72,621.82	81,833.21	4,462.11	4,982.54	3,332.04	2,212.06	57,158.44	59,774.77
2013	69,083.98	79,484.71	4,256.31	4,846.11	3,537.84	2,348.50	61,414.76	64,620.88
2014	65,327.63	76,991.36	4,037.81	4,701.26	3,756.35	2,493.35	65,452.56	69,322.14
2015	61,339.27	74,344.22	3,805.80	4,547.47	3,988.35	2,647.13	69,258.37	73,869.61
2016	57,104.58	71,533.82	3,559.47	4,384.20	4,234.69	2,810.40	72,817.84	78,253.81

Year	Loan Balance		Yearly Interest Paid		Yearly Principal Paid		Total Interest	
	Biweekly	Standard	Biweekly	Standard	Biweekly	Standard	Biweekly	Standard
2017	52,608.35	68,550.07	3,297.92	4,210.86	4,496.24	2,983.74	76,115.76	82,464.67
2018	47,834.41	65,382.30	3,020.22	4,026.83	4,773.94	3,167.77	79,135.98	86,491.50
2019	42,765.62	62,019.14	2,725.37	3,831.45	5,068.79	3,363.16	81,861.34	90,322.96
2020	37,383.76	58,448.56	2,412.30	3,624.02	5,381.86	3,570.59	84,273.64	93,946.97
2021	31,669.51	54,657.74	2,079.90	3,403.79	5,714.26	3,790.81	86,353.54	97,350.77
2022	25,602.32	50,633.12	1,726.97	3,169.98	6,067.19	4,024.62	88,080.52	100,520.75
2023	19,160.41	46,360.27	1,352.24	2,921.75	6,441.91	4,272.85	89,432.76	103,442.50
2024	12,320.62	41,823.87	954.37	2,658.21	6,839.79	4,536.39	90,387.13	106,100.72
2025	5,058.39	37,007.68	531.92	2,378.42	7,262.23	4,816.19	90,919.05	108,479.13
2026	0.00	31,894.44	107.13	2,081.37	5,058.39	5,113.24	91,026.18	110,560.50
2027	0.00	26,465.83	0.00	1,765.99	0.00	5,428.61	91,026.18	112,326.49
2028	0.00	20,702.39	0.00	1,431.17	0.00	5,763.44	91,026.18	113,757.66
2029	0.00	14,583.48	0.00	1,075.69	0.00	6,118.91	91,026.18	114,833.35
2030	0.00	8,087.16	0.00	698.29	0.00	6,496.32	91,026.18	115,531.64
2031	0.00	1,190.17	0.00	297.61	0.00	6,896.99	91,026.18	115,829.26
2032	0.00	0.00	0.00	8.93	0.00	1,190.17	91,026.18	115,838.19

10

Mmm ... A Taste for Luxury

YOUR FIRST THOUGHT WHEN looking at this chapter is, "Why are they telling me to spend money on luxuries when everything else in this book tells me to stop spending?" It's quite simple: deprivation leads to failure. That's right, when you deprive yourself entirely of something, the urge becomes stronger to sneak a taste of something or find a way to get back what you have been deprived of. How many times have you failed at a new diet? How many times when budgeting did you give up? How many times when saving money did you stop putting money aside because you felt like you were losing the quality of life by deprivation? The good news is that you can lose weight, stay on your budget, and save money by rewarding yourself. As you have read throughout this book, the key to financial success and wealth is to cut back, make a plan, and change old habits.

If you want the little luxuries of life, plan for it. For example, instead of shopping and stocking up on 10 pairs of shoes on sale, save your money for a good pair of shoes (a designer brand, if you want) and buy only one pair. The danger of grabbing the first pair of shoes on sale is that it's probably an impulse purchase. We know that happens, because we've done it! The reality is that the 10 pairs of shoes you purchased on sale added together will probably have cost you more than the one pair of designer shoes. What do you really want? It's your call.

There are choices. Do you want to be an impulsive shopper, throwing your money away because it feels good at the time, or do you want to have luxurious things by saving up for them? True, you may have fewer things by reverting to one good-quality item, but wouldn't you rather have that than many things that you rarely use and only make clutter? See how that works? Deprive yourself of everything and you will go crazy. Purchase one good luxury item and you feel like you have accomplished something without going into debt. You'll appreciate that item even more.

HOW TO FIND MONEY FOR LUXURY ITEMS

All right, you're probably saying, "Why work when I can't enjoy the little pleasures of life? I work hard and deserve more than stressing out over money." Or "Why spend all this time saving money when I can't spend it now?" The good news is that you can do both, save and spend, without going crazy. The problem is that most people don't know how to spend it properly. They get caught up in the instant gratification of "give it to me now." That's usually what creates the problem of too much debt and no future or retirement savings. You can't create wealth by spending money on the wrong things. Look at the examples we have in Chapter 2, "Money Calorie Counter," and Chapter 3, "Other Addictions." Here is an example of ways to save money and accrue savings from the Money Calorie Counter:

Plain Bagel with Cream Cheese

Item Name	Cost	Calories			Pounds		Yearly Cost	10% Interest Compounded Savings		
		Srv	Month	Year	Mth	Yr		5 Years	10 Years	20 Years
Plain Bagel	$0.69	300	6,500	78,000	2	22	$179.40	$1,157.68	$30.62.43	$11,352.56
Plain Cream Cheese	$1.30	90	1,950	23,400	1	7	$338.00	$2,181.14	$5,769.80	$21,388.89

If you opted to get your morning bagel without cream cheese, you would save $338 a year and potentially seven pounds. By simply cutting back, you can take the money saved and put a portion in your "luxury bucket." Base the money that you saved on what percentage you allocated for your luxury bucket. Don't move money into the luxury category until you have distributed the money into your "selected savings bucket." Will that luxury item still be there when you retire? Will you have overspent your money on multitudes of items without saving for the future and be forced to live in a tent because you have no savings? The choice is yours.

You also need to use caution when reaching out for your luxury item. It's important that you don't owe any credit card debt when going for the luxuries. Why?

Because the goal in reaching for your luxury item is to pay cash for it! If it's a large luxury item such as a car and you don't have the cash and you need to finance it, put a large down payment on it to get smaller payments. Finance it for the shortest period of time, and try to pay it off early.

If you are looking at a designer handbag, jewelry, a big-screen television, or anything else on your wish list, pay cash. Not credit. As you accumulate the money you are saving for your dream item, cut back on other things. For example, if there is a designer handbag that you desperately want and it costs $400, don't buy any other handbags. Put money aside for the bag you want and cut back on your other addictions: the gourmet lattes, weekly manicures and pedicures, vending machine sodas, candy bars, and whatever else you are splurging on. Notice: cut back, don't eliminate your buying altogether. In no time at all you will be able to take the money you have saved from not splurging and buy your handbag or whatever item you really want. We are creatures of habit—and spending habits are no different from other ones.

Here's an example of the things you purchase in a typical workday and how those items add up by the end of the work week:

Item	Cost	Calories
Mocha	$3.35	400
Soda	$0.75	200
Newspaper	$0.50	
Bagel/cream cheese	$1.99	390
Daily Total	$6.59 per day	990 per day
Weekly Total (5 days a week)	$32.95 per week	4,950 per week

$$\$32.95 \times 12 \text{ weeks} = \$395.40 \text{ (handbag money)}$$

Look at the calories you are saving too!

Don't forget to make sure you have put money aside toward your savings (5 to 10 percent of earnings).

DREAM LUXURY ITEMS

More and more people in the middle-income bracket are "trading up"—paying a premium for luxury items they value with high-end features, and compensating by "trading down" in other areas. In other words, they are opting to purchase expensive items by sacrificing in other areas.

What is your luxury desire? Is it a designer purse or shoes, an exotic family vacation, a big-screen TV, an expensive watch, or a luxury car? All of us have a secret dream luxury list. What is yours? Complete the Dream Luxury worksheet.

Sample Dream Luxury Worksheet

Luxury Item	Cost
Vacation	$2,500
Designer Handbag	$400
Luxury Car	$29,000
Other	

Dream Luxury Worksheet

Luxury Item	Cost

There are hundreds of common luxury items people go for; you probably have them written down on your worksheet. Here are some of the common ones:

- Designer clothes
- Designer handbags
- Designer shoes
- Electronics:
  - Big-screen TVs
  - Computers and computer equipment
- Expensive tools
- Expensive watches
- Fine dining
- Fine jewelry
- Season tickets for events
- Travel

Let's look at ways that you can afford some of the items on the list.

Traveling

If traveling is your luxury, you need to set up a travel fund. Determine if you want a yearly vacation or opt to travel every other year. Suppose you want to take a cruise to the Bahamas for 10 days and the cost is $2,500. This is a trip you want to schedule the following year. That gives you 12 months to plan and save. Divide the cost of the trip, which is $2,500, by 12 months, which equals $208.33. That is the amount you must put into a special luxury account each month. Look back to your Money Calorie Counter and addiction list to see where you can cut back and put that money aside each month for your trip. If you decide instead to take the trip in two years, you would have to save $104.17 each month for 24 months to pay for it. Is that realistic? It probably is, if you go back and are disciplined with your special saving account. Remember, you don't have to cut back everything, just enough for you to contribute to that special fund. You don't want to charge the trip on your credit card without the cash to pay it all off. When you are doing your calculations for the trip, don't forget to include in your savings fund extra spending for souvenirs. If you must use your credit card to secure your reservation, make sure you have the cash to pay it off right away and don't get charged interest.

ANN'S STORY

Ann loved to travel and take exotic trips. She made an average income and made choices on what she should spend her money on. Ann paid off her car and opted to keep it as long as she could. She took a portion of the money she once used for her car payment and put it in her travel fund as well as a special fund for her future car. Ann was driving a five-year-old car with the intent to drive the car until it died. She had 70,000 miles on the car.

By using this strategy, Ann was able to travel to most of the places she wanted to visit. She also had money set aside for her future car. Eventually, she hopes to pay cash or put a large down payment toward the car or pay it off as soon as possible.

You can use the same type of calculation on each luxury item you want. Have a goal for when you hope to make the purchase, and begin saving your money toward your luxury.

Everyone has different luxuries or indulgences. A luxury for one person may not be one for someone else. The cost for your item may not be very extravagant, but it may still be a stretch for you. Whatever your luxury is, expensive or not, make sure you plan for it, pay cash for it, and enjoy it.

Let's tackle a few more of the luxury items you may have on the list.

Designer Clothes, Designer Handbags, and Designer Shoes

These items can be clumped together. If you opt to buy designer apparel, think twice about it. Ask yourself, how long will the fashion and style be around? Is it trendy, or will it be outdated?

If you opt to purchase any of the items, make sure your investment will be able to be worn or used for many years to come and that it is a neutral item that won't be dated.

Suppose you find a pair of designer shoes that you must have. The cost is higher than what you usually spend—let's say $300. Look back at what your budget is for clothing each month. If it is $150 per month and you don't spend your clothing allowance on anything else, it will take you two months to buy the shoes by paying cash, or you can go back and see what you can cut out in other areas. Review your Money Calorie Counter journal to see what areas you can cut back on that month. This will expedite your purchase.

Before you make your purchase, check other stores and Web sites to see if you can purchase the items there at a lesser price. It's not uncommon for stores to offer different prices on the same item.

Expensive Watches and Jewelry

Most people love fine jewelry and expensive watches. They buy without planning for these purchases and end up owing large sums of money on their credit cards. If fine jewelry and expensive watches is your luxury item, plan for it. See where you can cut back from your list and save weekly and monthly until you have the money to pay cash. Visit jewelry marts and pawnshops to get a huge discount on the items. We have heard that some of the pawnshops have Rolex watches for half the price. Know what is good quality before making your purchase, and stop spending your money on the cheaper items. For what you pay for the cheaper items, you could have saved for the genuine fine jewelry and watch.

Fine Dining

Eating at expensive restaurants may be your luxury item. If you want to do this once a month or every three months, reflect where you can cut back. Review your Money Calorie Counter and addictions worksheet. You can take a small percentage of your food budget or entertainment allowance and add this to your luxury savings as well. Don't overindulge. Look for entertainment-type coupon books to use. Some offer two-for-one dinners at their fine dining restaurants.

If your luxury is tickets for a ball game or Broadway plays, careful planning is needed for season tickets. Usually season tickets are costly. Suppose the season tickets cost $800 for all the dates; you would need to save approximately $66.67 per month for 12 months to have the necessary amount. Reflect back to your list to see where you can cut back, and put the money each month into your special luxury account. Pay cash and don't charge.

Here's a goal sheet you can use for saving toward that luxury item you want.

Luxury Goal Sheet

Luxury Item	Cost	Monthly Amt. to Save	Months to Save Amount

11

Sharing Your Wealth

MOST PEOPLE HAVE THE desire to give money to their church, religious organization, charities, or people in need. Learning how to give is just as important as learning how to receive. There is a proverb that says, "A generous man will prosper; he who refreshes others will himself be refreshed" (Proverbs 11:25 NIV). What a truth in those words.

Being in a position to give money, whether you have a lot or very little, to help someone in need, or to contribute to your church or place of worship, a charitable organization, or some other needy cause, will open you up to receive blessings in your life. These blessings may not necessarily be returned as money. They could be good health, a great family, knowledge that you have helped someone in need, watching your church or place of worship spread money to help others or add to its building program. Or it could be simply knowing that your money was used to further medical research and a charitable cause.

Let's take a look at the Money Calorie Counter to see where you can find the extra money to give.

Turkey Sandwich

Item Name	Cost	Srv	Calories		Pounds		Yearly Cost	10% Interest Compounded Savings		
			Month	Year	Mth	Yr		5 Years	10 Years	20 Years
Turkey Sandwich	$3.39	330	7,150	85,800	2	25	$881.40	$5,687.75	$15,045.86	$55,775.64

Increase your donations to a nonprofit organization by $881.40 a year by using the money you would have spent on a turkey sandwich. You'll also avoid gaining 25 pounds in the process.

Even if you don't indulge in particular food items on a regular basis, you can refer back to your other addictions, but the point is that you can cut back on what you are spending and put aside an equivalent amount of money into your savings account. Refer back to Chapter 4, "Saving Money and Calories," to see where you can cut down. Eating meals out and buying gourmet drinks not only cost you money but will also add pounds to your figure. Finding ways to cut this type of spending will free up money so you can give more to organizations and people in need.

Refer to Chapter 3, "Other Addictions: Silent Money Thieves," to see where you can find even more money to give to your favorite charities.

The needs in this world are great. By donating in times where you have little money but give what you can, you will definitely be rewarded with blessings.

DEBORAH'S STORY

Many years ago when my three daughters were grade school age, we had been facing some financial challenges. It was Christmas time, and I began to think of what I had been thankful for during that year. It was health for my family. With the turbulent previous years and constant health problems with my children and family, I really was thankful for that one year. I began to think, "What can I do to help someone else in need?"

I contacted our local county hospital to see if there were any children who would be in the hospital during the Christmas holiday. The case worker said there were eight children who were terminally ill that would be in the hospital during that time. She wrote the ages of the boys and girls on the sheet of paper next to their names . . . plus she indicated a family of one of the children who was in great need.

I only had $100 to work with. That was all I could afford. This became a family project, and the goal was to get presents to those children before Christmas Eve.

My three daughters and I watched the newspapers daily for sales. And our shopping began. As we shopped for the gifts for the children, my daughters became so excited with the project that they each said, "Mom and Dad, don't buy us any Christmas presents this year. Use the money to buy more presents for the needy children."

After all the shopping was done, the family and I spent the evening individually wrapping the gifts for the children. We bought a gift certificate for food for the family in need as well. I don't know how we did it, but the $100 went a long way, and each child received more than one gift.

The next day I will never forget the sight of my husband, Hal, and the girls placing the presents in a large green trash bag and Hal slinging the trash bag over his shoulder like Santa Claus delivering the gifts to the hospital.

On Christmas Day, as my daughters opened their presents (we gave them gifts anyway, despite their requests not to), they would stop and each say at different times, "I wonder how the children liked their gifts?" It truly was a Christmas we will all remember and a blessing for each of us.

The blessings didn't stop that day. Two weeks after Christmas, we received in the mail a check for $100 from an overpayment from our insurance company that was unexpected.

It is my belief that we all were created to help others. You might say to yourself, "I don't have much, so how can I give money?" Well, if you don't have money, you have time. Volunteer your time to the church, place of worship, or charity that you want to help. That is giving. Your time is worth money. Give money when you can.

I know when my money was plentiful, I was able to give more money to helping others. What

amazed me, though, was that when we hit a financial slump and had little money, we were blessed by
others. Most people never knew our financial pitfall.
There would be times when we would be asked to
go out to dinner with another couple and be reluctant to go, when out of nowhere the couple would
say, "We want you to be our guests for dinner."
Another time, when I went along with my sister
Cathy while she shopped, Cathy stopped and said,
"This dress would look great on you. I want to get it
for you." These are truly blessings.

What I have found is that when you have plenty
of money and you give to others, and there comes
a time in your life when your money supply is low,
someone will give back to you. It's why we were created. To give.

To help you find money, or to budget your money, go
back through your worksheets and journal to see where
there has been some wasted spending. Check the Money
Calorie Counter to see where you can cut the calories and
save money. Also go over your other addictions. If you
have change you are throwing in a box, count it at the end
of each month and give it away. You'll be surprised how
much that can add up.

It's true that it is easier to give than to receive.
Sometimes you may feel uncomfortable receiving something unexpected, especially if you are going through hard
times, but know this: the one giving is being blessed too.

When a friend, family member, or stranger gives you a gift or money, welcome it. Let that person know how much you appreciate it. Remember, what goes around, comes around. You are blessed.

HOW TO GIVE

At the beginning of every month, allocate how much you want to give each month. It is recommended that you give 10 percent of your income. If you can't handle that much, allocate what you can. Giving something is better than nothing.

Next, write out your check at the beginning of each month, if possible, to the organization or person to whom you want to donate. That way, when you have given it will always be clear in your mind, and you will have formed a good habit. If that doesn't work for you, write out the check when you can.

GIVING FROM THE HEART

Many times you will be moved to give from the heart for an immediate cause or person in need and not receive a tax deduction. You don't want to have the attitude of giving only for receiving. If you do that, you have the wrong attitude. Look at giving as an extension of your time or money to see how it makes a difference.

There may be times when you feel that a person or organization may need some financial help. That may be the time you need to give without knowing the reason why.

DEBORAH'S STORY

When I started my business and received my first order, I was inspired to give that money to a friend of ours overseas who was a missionary. Even though I had not seen her for several years and without knowing why, I mailed the check. A couple of years later, when she was back in town, she came to our home and visited. She indicated that the day she received the check, she had picked up the mail and gone to a dental appointment without opening the letter. She had to have dental work done and didn't know how she was going to pay for it. As she waited in the dentist's office, she opened the letter, and there was the check. She couldn't believe her eyes. It was enough to pay for all the dental work. She was blessed, and years later when I heard the story, I was blessed too.

MELINDA'S STORY

A few years ago, one of my friends was struggling financially. One day, she made a comment to me that all she could afford to eat were noodles and soup that she made at home. Later, I thought about our conversation. In my heart I knew I needed to help my friend. I also knew that she wouldn't accept my money. So, I decided to buy her groceries. I showed up at her house with bags of groceries. You should have seen her face!

DEBORAH'S STORY

I had just finished being interviewed on Warren Duffy's *Live From L.A.* show, a live radio call-in program. When I returned to my office, there was a telephone message from Todd, who had heard the show. He asked that I call him back.

When I returned Todd's call, he indicated that he and his wife, Mary, had been greatly moved by a caller who was going through serious financial problems and needed advice. The caller's name was Jill.

Jill had shared her story with the radio host and I on how she was having trouble paying her bills. Her husband was in a wheelchair on a medical disability. She needed medicine for her family; her tires were bald; she was holding two jobs and couldn't pay all her bills.

Todd and Mary were so moved by her story that they wanted to give Jill $500 to help her. They wanted me to be the go-between.

I explained to Todd that when being interviewed on a radio show, the caller's telephone number usually is not given, but I would contact the producer to see what could be done to try to find Jill. It didn't seem possible. It was like trying to find a needle in a haystack.

I called Duffy's producer and explained the situation. The next day, Duffy got on the air and made an announcement that we were looking for Jill who called the show the previous day and instructed her to call back.

That evening, the producer called me back to let me know they thought they had found Jill. He gave me her phone number to call the following day.

When I got ahold of Jill, I asked her several questions before I told her why I was looking for her. I was concerned we would get the wrong person. As we talked, I was satisfied that she was the right person. I asked Jill if she had heard the announcement the previous night looking for her. She said she had not. A friend of hers was driving home from work and was playing a CD. The CD popped out of the holder and the radio came on at the precise time Duffy made the announcement looking for Jill. Her friend realized it was Jill and called Jill's husband. He said that Jill had called the show the previous day and he called the producer. What a small miracle!

Todd and Mary wanted to remain anonymous, so I told Jill that they wanted to give her family $500.

Jill became very quiet and began to cry. I was so touched that I began to cry too. She quietly whispered, "I feel like a butterfly that has just been released to fly." I told her that Todd and Mary wanted her to use the money for tires, medicine, and things that were pertinent to survival.

The next day, Jill called me back and told me that her husband had been in a great depression. When he heard what Todd and Mary wanted to do, he felt there was hope, and his confidence was renewed.

Todd and Mary sent the money to me to forward to Jill and her husband. What a blessing for all those involved.

The great thing about this story is that there are people like Todd and Mary who are looking for people like Jill to help. I was blessed to be a part of this ... as were Duffy and his producer and those who heard the story. The blessing spilled all over.

Giving can be a wonderful way to feel good about yourself. There's a saying that what you give, you receive. We believe this to be true. When you give and know that it's needed and appreciated, the feeling it gives you is priceless. Remember that it's the collected efforts of individuals, like you and us, that make the difference for all kinds of people and causes in need.

OUR FAVORITE CHARITIES

Here is a list of some of the charities that we like to contribute to. They are all worthwhile causes, reputable organizations, and in need of support. You may find others that you find are equally worthwhile, but these are a good starting point in your efforts to give.

American Cancer Society
1599 Clifton Road, NE
Atlanta, GA 30329
800-227-2345
www.cancer.org

American Heart Association
7272 Greenville Avenue
Dallas, TX 75231-4596
800-242-8721
www.americanheart.org

American Red Cross
2025 E Street, NW
Washington, DC 20006
(202) 737-8300
www.redcross.org

Big Brothers Big Sisters of America
National Headquarters, 230 North 13th Street
Philadelphia, PA 19107-1510
215-567-7000
www.bbbsa.org

Compassion International
12290 Voyager Parkway
Colorado Springs, CO 80921

800-336-7676
www.compassion.com

Habitat for Humanity International
121 Habitat Street
Americus, GA 31709-3498
800-422-4828
www.habitat.org

Make-A-Wish Foundation of America
3550 North Central Avenue, Suite 300
Phoenix, AZ 85012-2107
800-722-9474
www.wish.org

Project Impact USA
2640 Industry Way, Suite G
Lynwood, CA 90262
(888) 242-2778
www.projectimpactusa.org

Salvation Army
P.O. Box 269
615 Slaters Lane
Alexandria, VA 22313
703-684-5500
www.salvationarmyusa.org

Susan G. Komen Breast Cancer Foundation
5005 LBJ Freeway, Suite 250
Dallas, TX 75244
800-462-9273
www.komen.org

Conclusion

WE DON'T MIND TELLING YOU that as we were writing this book, it became an eye-opener to us in our own personal lives. After writing this book and researching the little indulgences and other addictions we sometimes partake of, we are both in agreement that when shopping, we need to put blinders on our eyes and evaluate if we really "need it." We know if it can change our lives, it will also change yours.

We have given you the tools to slim your waistline, grow your bank account, and build personal wealth. It just takes discipline and a plan to do that. All the things you have wanted to do—lose weight, grow your checkbook, get out of debt, get healthier, and give to charities—are now at your fingertips. So are our tips for a few "luxuries" you might want to indulge in.

Take this book with you and use it as a guide to improve your diet and fatten your checkbook. Don't be impulsive or tempted to fall back into old habits.

Our Money Calorie Counter is not meant to deprive you of ever eating a chocolate bar, or having the latte you are craving, or purchasing that favorite CD. It is meant to make you aware of what you are spending your money on, and how you can cut back to save and build wealth. It is also meant to enlighten you on the calories you are taking in with food or beverages that really are not the best things for you or the high cost you are paying for these things.

By utilizing the information in this book, you can become debt free, start a great savings account, lose weight, and maintain a healthy lifestyle. You can have it all.

We would love to hear from you and hear about your success and tips. Also, we would love to send you our free monthly newsletter. Visit us at: www.richandthinliving .com or e-mail us at info@richandthinliving.com. When you visit our Web site, be sure to take a look at our fun products and tools!

Index

About the Authors

Deborah McNaughton is a nationally recognized credit expert and financial coach. She has been in the financial business for over 25 years. Deborah has been in the financial business since 1984 and is the founder of Financial Victory Institute, which specializes in credit and financial education. Deborah is a  licensed real estate broker and has over 30 years of experience. With her husband Hal she also co-owns Legacy Financial Services, which specializes in mortgages.

Deborah has authored several books about credit and finances. Some of her books include, *The Get Out Of Debt Kit* (Kaplan Business), *Financially Secure: An Easy-to-Follow Money Program for Women* (Thomas Nelson Publishers), *All about Credit: Questions and Answers about the Most Common Credit Problems* (Kaplan Business), and *The Insider's Guide to Managing Your Credit* (Kaplan Business and Berkley Publishing). She has coauthored a book with John Avanzini titled, *Have a Good Report*. Recently, Deborah has released a new financial series titled *Financial Victory*, which consists of booklets, CDs, and pamphlets on numerous financial issues. This series is available online at www.financialvictory.com.

Deborah is a monthly financial columnist for *First for Women*, which has a circulation of approximately two million. Several magazines and newspapers have featured and quoted Deborah including *Parade, Woman's Day, Your Money, Success Opportunities, Working Woman, Today's Christian Woman*, and *Income Opportunities*. The *New York Times, Wall Street Journal, Chicago Tribune*, and several other news publications have quoted Deborah numerous times as an authority on credit. Deborah currently produces a free monthly newsletter titled *Financial Victory*, which has over 3,000 subscribers. For more information about the *Financial Victory* newsletter and Deborah's services, visit her Web site at www.financial victory.com.

Deborah has been interviewed on hundreds of television and radio stations around the country. She has been a guest on CNN, CNN-FN, Bloomberg Television, *Good Day New York, Lifetime New Attitudes*, and many other television programs. Deborah is the radio host of *The Money Manager* program, a radio show designed to help individuals with their personal finances.

Thousands of people have benefited from the financial advice that Deborah provides through her books, seminars, interviews, and newsletters. Deborah's sincere desire is to educate and empower people on how to take control of their finances.

Melinda Weinstein is the cofounder of Financial Victory Institute, which specializes in credit and financial education. Melinda is the managing editor of *Financial Victory*, a popular online financial newsletter. She is a regular columnist for a specialty magazine, *Woman's Touch*—a bimonthly publication with a circulation

of approximately fourteen thousand subscribers. Melinda is the coauthor of the *Financial Victory* series, which consists of numerous financial booklets and pamphlets.

Melinda was in charge of *A Gift for America: How to Survive a Financial Crisis* project, which consists of a financial video, educational Web site, and monthly online newsletter. She has contributed financial articles to the educational Web site of a national debt management company.

Melinda has been quoted in various magazines as a credit expert, including *Woman's World*, a weekly publication that has a circulation of approximately 1.6 million. She has also been interviewed on radio regarding credit and financial matters. Melinda has over nine years of experience in the mortgage industry and five years devoted to credit counseling. She has had her real estate license for the last three years. Melinda has a Master of Business Administration from Arizona State University. She is Deborah McNaughton's daughter.